MAK MUSIC SPECIAL

Practical Ways to Create Music

JOHN CHILDS

David Fulton Publishers
London

David Fulton Publishers Ltd
2 Barbon Close, London WC1N 3JX

First published in Great Britain by
David Fulton Publishers 1996

Note: The right of the author to be identified as the author of this work has been asserted by him in accordance with the Copyright, Designs and Patents Act 1988.

Copyright © John Childs

British Library Cataloguing in Publication Data

A catalogue record for this book is available from the British Library

ISBN 1-85346-417-1

All rights reserved. No part of this publication may be reproduced, stored in a retrieval system or transmitted in any form, or by any means, electronic, mechanical, photocopying, recording or otherwise, without the prior permission of the publishers.

Typeset by The Harrington Consultancy, London
Printed in Great Britain by BPC Books & Journals Ltd. Exeter

Contents

Introduction and Acknowledgements		v
Chapter 1	The General Direction	1
Chapter 2	Ways Into Making Music Special	8
Chapter 3	Moving on to Make Music Special	24
Chapter 4	Increasing Sophistication	45
Chapter 5	Special Learners	69
Chapter 6	Developing Creativity and Imagination	86
Chapter 7	Personal Musical Development	98
Chapter 8	Organisation and Resources to Make Music Special	112
Appendix 1	The Relationship of Notes in Musical Scales	122
Appendix 2	Musical Examples	124
Appendix 3	Common Chords	126
Further Reading		128
Index		129

For Ann

Introduction and Acknowledgements

Making Music Special has become more technical than I first envisaged. My intention is to provide only the theoretical background necessary to an understanding of students' developmental progression. Do not feel daunted by this approach.

My teaching experience has been with every category of student. Within the course of a week, personal music sessions will take place in disparate teaching situations. These can range from adults in long-term psychiatric care to children in nursery education. Primary schools, able pupils and professional artists are part of my full schedule. I have discovered that all of my students are searching for, and responding to, similar ways of presenting musical content. It is my practical experience that provides the substantive knowledge base for this book.

It is difficult to represent the pleasure, fun and laughter reflected and remembered in the music-making sessions. I deliberately attempt to adopt a colourful approach! Fun and laughter have always been the bedrock of all aspects of my work. May I also at this point confess to a total intolerance towards systems which deliberately distress, frighten or threaten children. We all understand the negative influences of sadness and duress. Happy and animated pupils provide and encourage the best teaching.

Carl Rogers, an American psychologist, has had a deep influence on my work. A one-sentence summary of my philosophy would be: a person-centred approach, reflected in congruence, acceptance and empathy.

I offer a few words of thanks to the many friends and colleagues who have helped to make this book possible. The first words are an expression of gratitude to the young people in schools maintained by Nottinghamshire County Council Education Committee. The schools have proved to be a stimulating musical laboratory and the pupils a continual source of motivation and inspiration. Memories of some individuals are burnished into my brain. Lisa, Polly, Matthew, Joanne, David, Darren, Mark, Zieh. Some of these young people experienced learning difficulties and could communicate only in limited ways, yet they taught me many great lessons. Thank you to Mrs Kim Glossop for deciphering my scrawl and typing it into the computer. Finally a huge amount of thanks to Ann Childs. She has laboured over the script with me at every stage with tolerance and understanding, all well beyond the call of matrimonial duty.

Please accept the following pages as an open and honest handbook to help all of you create music. I hope you will continue to dip into its pages for some time to come.

Enjoy *Making Music Special!*

John Childs
May 1996

CHAPTER 1

The General Direction

This book is powered by my deep desire to present both the techniques and philosophy of open access music making. Working with music can be highly challenging but it is also an exciting factor in the personal development and motivation of many young people. Music is a language closely associated with our deep emotions and feelings, but it possesses the power to communicate beyond our spoken and written language. Music should never be placed at the margins or considered to be frivolous. Every expressive tool requires common access as a right and demands we portray it in a welcoming style.

The ideas, techniques and opinions found here are all about open access to music, a brilliant art form providing incalculable benefit to our human way of life. The clear relationship between early music making and advanced musical performance requires careful examination; this is further explored throughout the pages. On one level, music is a highly technical subject; on another, it is a simple art form that is part of our very existence.

Once the individuals, or their teacher, start making music they need a sense of direction – where is the music going and why is it going that way? This sense of direction is a difficult notion and is an area of controversy amongst music educators, some of whom are content with closed situations. We tend to look and hope for simplistic structures, but the reality is a very complex and mixed progression.

Developing languages

There is an interesting relationship between the acquisition of spoken language and music development. Frequently the ideas expressed in this book reflect a philosophical slant towards this relationship. The idea works in a very natural way: infants watch how words are formed, listen to language, experiment with sounds and attempt to imitate their language models. By continual practice and trials they acquire the language skills to express their thoughts, ideas and wishes.

> Watch – Listen – Experiment – Copy – Communicate

Surrounding adults and other children, often unwittingly, provide a supportive environment to sustain the efforts of their young 'language learner' by providing copious signs of approval, being 'tuned in' to early words, attributing sense to what is 'said' and ignoring or appreciating the nonsensical aspects of trying. This approach works and has to be the most common open access strategy. It is used by people from every cultural background. The same model is used for learning other languages; it can become equally effective in developing the language of music. (Reading and writing follow on at a later stage within this plan.)

A thoughtful examination of how people learn is required. Working with those who experience learning difficulties often presents insights into how we can effectively influence the learning process. These students demand that we reflect carefully on our own teaching styles and encourage a sharper focus on how to best approach this thing called 'learning'. Once adopted, this attentive examination of learning processes serves us exceptionally well for teaching all students. It opens our eyes to our potential to further develop our thoughts and ideas.

How We Learn

There are a few simple ways we all learn. The mental processes are complex, but the methods remarkably obvious. We learn by employing some of the following strategies:

Experimenting	Examples	Participating
Interacting	Role Playing	Information
Games	Reading	Experiences
Imitating	Observing	Trying things out
Problem solving	Listening	Making mistakes
Role models	Asking questions	Watching
Touching	Direct teaching	Discussing
Memorising	Investigating	Playing hunches

All of these require encouragement, praise and confidence to build motivation, success and enjoyment. These are the strong influences that nourish our students.

Teachers must take control of their own musicality. Music is not in the hands of others. This book is designed to help you take control. My intention is not to provide a series of instant ideas for music sessions, although there are numerous ideas for individual development. Ultimately you address your own needs and the needs of the young people in your group. Develop the ideas to make them your own. Experiment with ways of adapting materials to make them appropriate for the age and ability of your young people.

Remember:

- Musical development is accomplished by doing.
- Do not wait to be gifted. Most musical work is the result, as the saying goes, of a high degree of perspiration and a very small portion of inspiration.
- Music making is emotionally demanding. This can make you vulnerable to feelings of inadequacy. (Most musicians want to be better musicians.)

Approaching This Book

This book will interest all who are, in the broadest sense, taking on the role of 'teacher'. I imagine its readers will include teachers, parents, carers, therapists and other professionals. Some may be able enthusiasts whilst others are specialists. The open access approach provides encouragement for everyone to develop their musical potential, with or without any previous background. Technical items are explained in simple terms, and although this inevitably results in some compromises it does avoid a morass of musical jargon.

Be enthusiastic. This is the great contributing factor towards musical success. Previous experience playing an instrument is not an essential qualification, but those who are seeking to develop their playing skills should appreciate the information given in Chapter 7.

This book always refers to the client group as 'young people'. This is used as a generic term and is intended to include everyone who is developing their music making. References to young people with learning difficulties also takes account of the range of educational provision, from specialist settings through to integration within a neighbourhood school. Teachers should always seek opportunities to provide avenues for all young people to reach their full potential and to recognise the broad spectrum of ability within any group.

Significant group differences are addressed by teaching techniques designed to be:

- consistent
- well directed
- flexible in nature
- reflective towards individuals
- motivated by encouragement and fair praise
- enjoyable
- possessing reachable objectives.

Your enthusiasm, commitment and professional judgement can create an exciting world of music for everyone. Be alongside the people in your care and be ready to learn from their diversity and richness.

National Curriculum

The broad outline of this book follows the structure used in the Music National Curriculum (1995) for creating music, although the NC attempts to be more linear in its progression. (Chapter 2 relates to Key Stage 1; Chapter 3 to Key Stage 2; and implications for Key Stage 3 are included in Chapter 4.) However, you are encouraged to 'dip in' at any point you feel is suitable to your needs. The National Curriculum should not restrict more advanced explorations. Do not hold back if your young people have a thirst to gain deeper levels of understanding.

The composition ideas throughout the book will be of interest to all early composers, regardless of level or background. Importantly, remember how events are relevant to a specific order; advanced information is part of the natural progression required to achieve deeper levels of musical improvisation. Often our aim should be to promote young people to become the equivalent of fluent thinkers and speakers in the language of music. Adopt strategies designed to make your young people conversational both in music playing and musical thinking.

If your group missed out on early musical experiences or need further early work, then early work is the place to start; this should not be considered juvenile or unsophisticated. There is a profound difference between where young people are and where we would wish them to be. Early and relatively raw musical experiences can be presented in a way to make them meaningful and expressive.

During their early years young people can easily lose their musicality by a chance negative remark, often uttered by a significant adult. Many genuine, positive comments in highly supportive surroundings are needed to compensate for lost confidence. Sometimes our attempts will encompass a desire to re-build lost musicality. It is not uncommon for people to quickly consider themselves as 'no good at music'; our approach should attempt to redress these attitudes. Aim to build a supportive environment at all times. Early experiences will involve 'falling over'; the role of the adult is to pick the individual up, dust them down and lead them along a safe and supportive pathway.

Scan the pages. Find those things of interest to you. Develop concepts for yourself and your group. Get on and do it. Review what you have done and then move on. This journey has purpose and direction. To make music is the opening gambit!

The Ingredients of Music

What is music and what are its constituent parts? It could be argued that music education contains the following parts:

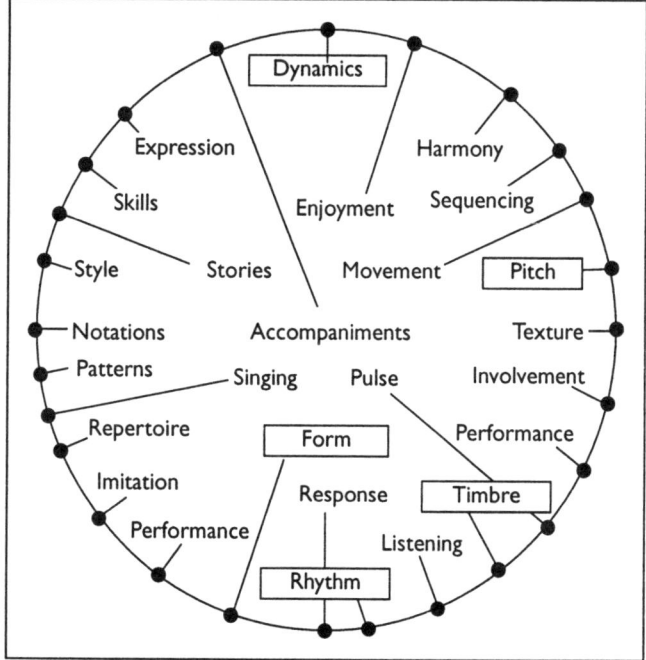

Constituent Parts of Music Education

This crowded list may see overwhelming. Focus on a few of the essential elements required for making music. Those outlined in boxes are the most important.

Music is reliant upon these component parts for its very being; we must establish a firm understanding of them in order to handle and make sense of music. Teachers require a general notion of how these ingredients work, both at an individual level and also in response to each other. This is accomplished by focusing first on each ingredient. It is impossible to totally isolate any single component since each one has many variables and each presents a potential for music to fluctuate between simplicity and complexity. The relationship between components and their variables lies close to the heart of music making. Since rhythm and pitch are the most complex they will take up a major proportion of our time, effort and energy.

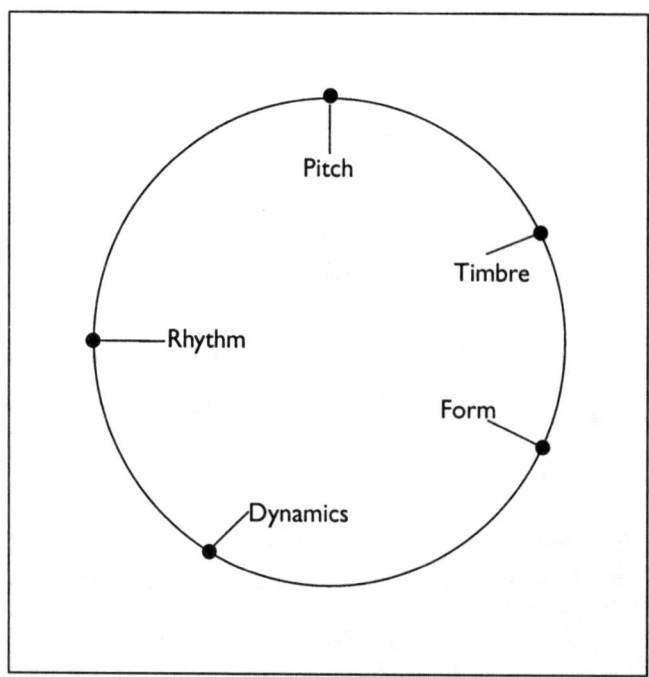

Basic Ingredients of Music

The Progression

If we extract one ingredient – pitch – a new sideways view reveals its development along a spiral route:

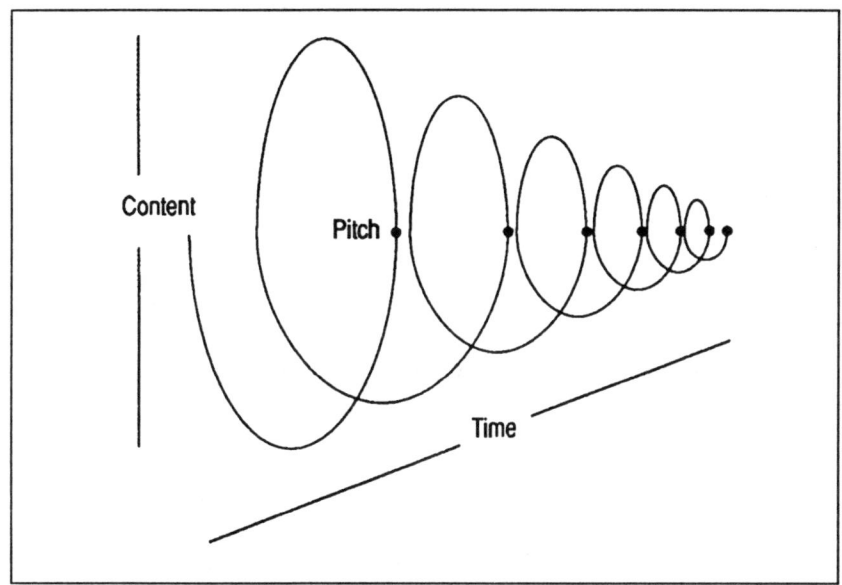

A Musical Flume: the spiral of progression

The progression – sliding along this musical flume – illustrates the method by which musical ingredients are revisited each time we tumble around its walls. On each re-visit we seek to add new information. Other human attributes associated with the passing of time will also come into play such as maturation, experience, motor control, technique and knowledge.

We all embark on a journey through music possessed of helter-skelter images: routes cross and change direction, we come back on ourselves, move around in circles and re-visit elements – all in a spiral of interaction. The book draws on this metaphor of spiral development and at the same time encourages the teaching of skills, techniques and ideas. Individuals process this information, and subsequently amalgamate it into their own musical creations.

This happy, exciting and challenging journey is yours to make.

CHAPTER 2

Ways Into Making Music Special

The musical ingredients established in Chapter 1 – timbre, beat/pulse, dynamics, rhythm, pitch – are now discussed in more detail. In this chapter the key musical components are defined and ideas for facilitating their practical use provided.

Timbre: Quality of Sound

Music making is the process of organising different sounds. Vibrations

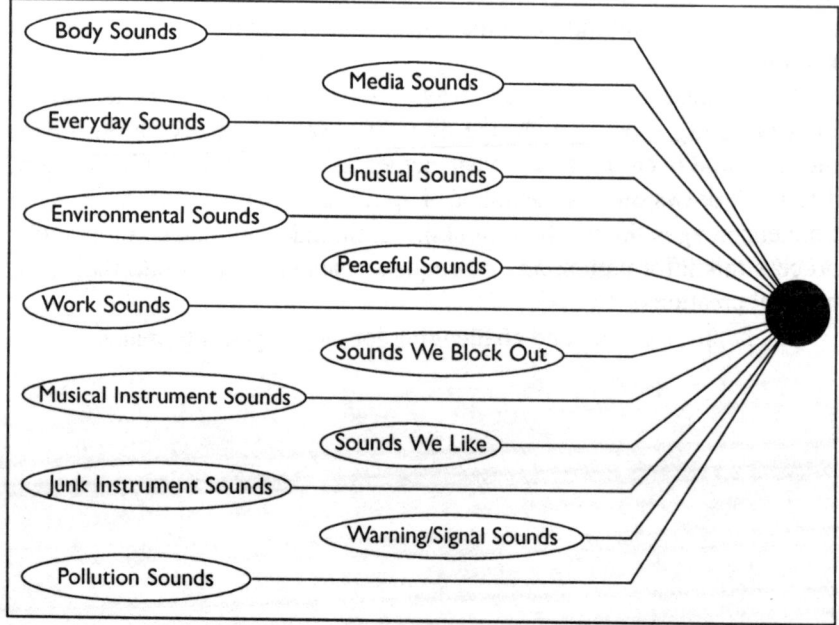

Sorting Sounds

are all around us most of the time. Become aware of those sounds we can take hold of and control in an organised way.

I use the expression 'interesting sounds' because we are then taking account of sounds which may not be 'nice' or 'beautiful', but all sounds have a potential for music making. Consider several different categories of sounds available to our ears. Maybe you will have some headings of your own to add. From these headings, it becomes reasonable to draw up your own lists of those items within the experience of your young people. Each heading could be expanded in this way:

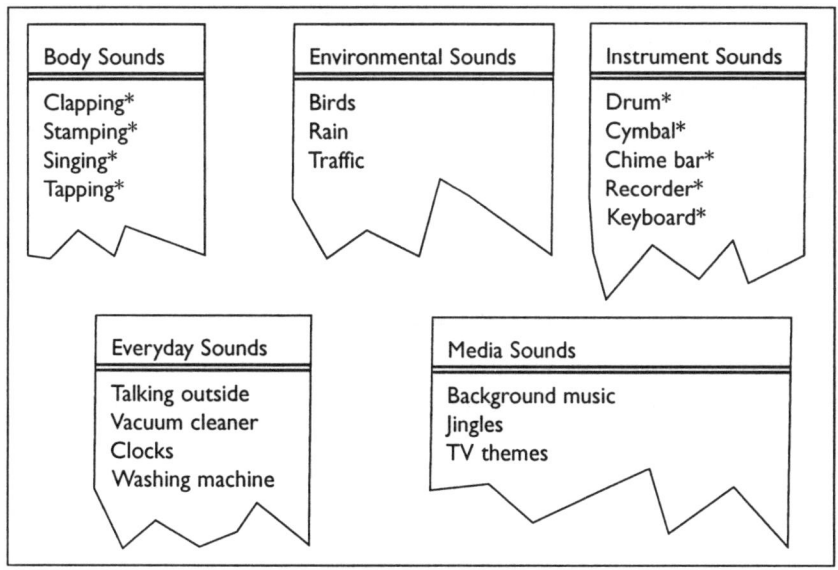

Sound Sources

The symbol (*) indicates those sounds we have some immediate control over, an important consideration. Because variety is important, this process should be the starting point for building resources of sounds. Consider making collections of sounds – from natural items, from everyday objects, things to shake, and so on.

Electronic equipment allows sounds to be recorded, organised and modified – a way of controlling sounds which initially are outside our control. Tape recorders can be used to make sound collections; additional hi-tech music equipment makes it possible to re-shape these sounds and provide timbre experiences for more advanced music students (Chapter 3).

Direct experience of handling and controlling sound is important. Doing is infinitely more valuable than talking about doing. The richer forms of learning appeal to several senses at the same time. These are the most direct channels to the brain, the way we perceive and construct what is happening in the outside world. Those experiences which are direct and firsthand are the most vivid; we should actively pursue them for our young musicians.

Spend plenty of time handling sounds, allowing everyone to experiment with sound. There are no fixed rules, even when handling orthodox musical instruments. We must accept each individual contribution in a constructive way, a way that values ideas. When ideas are accepted and given worth then more ideas start to flow. Open-ended thoughts are valuable, we need to encourage their proliferation. A dialogue might go something like this:

- Show me how you made that interesting sound on your tambourine.
- How are you making that sound?
- Well done! Does it remind you of anything? It reminds me of the rain.

Sorting Sounds

Here are some ideas for experimenting with sound qualities:

- Everyone chooses an instrument to play.
- Find different ways of playing the instrument to obtain a variety of sounds.
- Use words to describe the quality of the sound.
- Explore ways of dividing into related groups:
  – shakers, bangers, scrapers, twangers.
  – metallic, wood, skin, wind, plastic.
  – short or long sounding.
  – loud or quiet sounding.
  – large instruments or small instruments.
- Talk about, share and generally become immersed in timbre. Establish a strong general notion of sound qualities.

Ask the young people for suggestions at every opportunity. All are equally valid and acceptable. In response to their ideas do not forget to make ample use of positive feedback in order to build positive self images. ('That's a good answer', 'That's interesting', 'I've not thought about that before').

Imparting Meaning to Our Playing

Instrument playing and sound exploration should begin to establish some sense of expressing moods and messages. Music is an expressive language that helps us to make sense of our world and ourselves. All music needs to have some sense of purpose and meaning. Aim to establish simple meanings (originating from the young people) and to use broad brush strokes at this stage. Likely responses could be: shakers – sugar on cereals; drums – road repairs; metallic sounds – stars at night; short sounds – rain dripping from the trees; long sounds – busy traffic on a motorway.

The meanings given to a piece of musical sound are exposed to personal interpretation and poetic licence. A piece of musical sound is to be differentiated from a specific sound effect, which tends to be more restrictive in nature. Some musical instruments are purely sound effects; it is impossible for them to be anything else. A cuckoo call will always be a cuckoo call, whereas a recorder could play music in any context including a cuckoo impersonation on the notes **c** and **a**.

Stops and Starts

Once our instruments are playing we require a system to start and stop the music. Conducting is the usual convention for controlling players, if they are able to watch a conductor at the same time as playing an instrument. Not everyone immediately achieves this. The last persons to be playing could cue themselves from a neighbour by means of peripheral vision. Less restrictive systems can be explored:

- Traffic lights: two coloured circles, green held up to start playing and red to stop.
- Red and green gloves: similar to traffic lights.
- Puppet: play as it dances, stop when still.
- Torch: play when lit, stop when it is off.
- Baton: signals using a conducting stick.
- Statues: a person is moving or still.

Let the young people take charge of this whenever possible.

Once music is happening there is something to work on and develop. Establishing this process is similar to overcoming the forces of friction: providing the initial impetus requires most energy.

There will be times when the musical potential of an instrument only becomes apparent when one member of the group observes another young person playing it. Allow for plenty of instrument changes within a session. Present opportunities to permit legitimate ways of exchanging instruments and testing out ideas.

Controlling sounds is a never-ending task. The composer of a film score is continually searching for interesting sounds to enhance dramatic action. Sometimes the aural interest is achieved by combining several sounds. Listen to the way sound is employed musically in film scores. Music and sounds are extensively used to manipulate the emotional state of the viewer and enhance visual images (a vital part of TV cartoons). Create 'film scores' of your own in an encouraging atmosphere. Offer support to creative experimentation. Maintain a tangible relationship between aural and visual images by remaining within the realm of your young people's understanding.

The Piano as a Sound Source

A piano is a valuable and dramatic sound source, and only a small amount of preparation is required. Close the lid on the keys, remove the bottom cover to reveal the strings and find something suitable to wedge down the right hand (sustain) pedal. Sit facing the strings and experiment with a variety of vocal sounds. The piano strings gently vibrate in sympathy with the utterances, resulting in an echo effect. A transducer can be added to the piano sound board (the wood behind the strings). (See Chapter 4.)

Using the fingers stroke across the piano strings, or slide up and down the coarse textured bass strings. Tap on the sound board or pluck the short ends of each string. Soft beaters can also be used.

The piano sounds are long and ethereal, and lend themselves to mysterious music making. Perhaps useful music to describe:

- Dinosaur Times.
- Under the Sea.
- Landing on Mars.
- The Mysterious Forest.

Always work in the bottom of a piano away from the hammers; the action in the top of the instrument is not capable of withstanding this type of work. Grand pianos protect their delicate mechanisms underneath the strings so are safe to use in a similar fashion. Using the piano in this way is an example of inventiveness providing access to an instrument capable of a wealth of musical sound independent of any keyboard skills.

Before moving on to the next musical ingredient, it is prudent to remind the reader of the continual challenge to be inventive and to modify each idea to make it your own. Start a musical ideas note book – something small, so that it can be close at hand for jotting down useful information and ideas for the future.

Musical Pulse (as a prologue to rhythm)

The music composed up to this point has been free of any pulse. We now move on to explore the use of beat. (Remember it does not have to be an essential part of our musical creations.) Pulse, or beat, is a regular, even quality in music, a unit of time. It is similar to the pulse of our heart (beating 80 to 90 beats per minute). Just as our pulse rate increases as we become more active, so does the beat in music. Foot-tapping, movement and dancing are all a direct response to our detection of a regular pulse. The speed of music is measured by the number of beats per minute, exactly as our pulse is measured by the number of heart beats per minute.

	Beats per minute
Heart Beat	80 to 90
Walking Music	90 to 110
Running Music	120 to 230
Dance Rock Music	110 to 200

Regular Pulse Speeds

Pulse is naturally related to physical movement, bonding the two aspects together. Useful work involves exploring the connection. Walking has a natural, steady and even pulse, and so provides a good starting point. Young people can synchronise their ability to respond to a beat by looking and listening; very often they can be too eager to leap in and play. Our senses measure the space between each pulse; the most perceptive of us will need to hear three of four regular beats before we can synchronise our actions to it. Use improvisation to establish strong pulse/beat music. Allow time for people to climb aboard the pulse and synchronise their internal clock mechanisms. Build up beat playing ideas in this manner:

Walking to the bus stop

- Someone walks around in a steady, even way.
- One person picks up playing the beat in time to the walk.
- Use hand signals to bring in and include other players, one or a few at a time.
- Use a signal to stop together.

The space between each sound is of great importance. There is a strong tendency to make each consecutive gap smaller; this results in the music becoming faster and faster, sometimes a response to increased excitement.

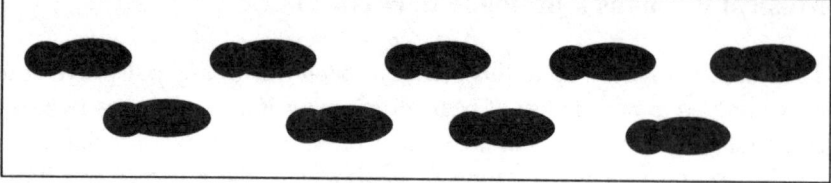

A Regular Pulse

Printed music often gives an indication of speed by using beats per minute [♩ = 120]. Italian words indicate speed:
Andante = walking speed
Allegro = fast speed
Prestissimo = fastest speed possible.

A music dictionary will give you a plentiful supply of other speed indicators, words signifying a broad range of speeds.

Metronomes (mechanical or electronic) establish the musical pace. Find one and explore its possibilities. Most of the latest electronic keyboards display the speed of the rhythm unit. The display registers beats per minute, an elaborate metronome.

Explore a variety of beats/pulses by improvising pieces of music related to different speeds. Some suggestions are:

- An amble in the park
- Marching down the main street
- Hurrying to the shops
- A cross country race

Add your own ideas.

You have introduced timbre and pulse. Now combine them. The permutations become vast.

Look back at the ideas above and consider how the tonal quality of the instruments could be used to further effect. Marching down the main street could be placed in the context of Roman soldiers. The choice of instruments – drums and tambours, plus a few small metal instruments (hints of armour and weapons) – colours the musical picture. Hurrying to the shops may include harsh sounds from instruments made of wood – short, sharp and rapid sounds indicating the frenzied hustle and bustle of a busy town. The cross country race may take us through cornfields with swishing sounds produced on maracas and the rainmaker; this in turn changes to a crisp sound of gravel in a plastic container. These are examples to initially stimulate thoughts; better ones will be invented by your young people. Always try to relate to direct experiences or to link with other areas of study.

Dynamics – Volume (loud/quiet)

Volume requires consideration at all stages of music making. The terms we use to express volume are relative, requiring our ears to play a game of comparison, i.e. loud music contrasting with quiet passages. The parameters of volume within our world may reveal at one extreme a bird fluttering its wings, at the other a jet aircraft taking off. The dynamic contrasts in music are thankfully more subtle in range. Once again Italian words are the musical convention used to indicate volume levels:

Very quiet	Quiet	Moderately quiet	Moderately loud	Loud	Very loud
pp	p	mp	mf	f	ff
pianissimo	piano	mezzopiano	mezzoforte	forte	fortissimo

Indicators of Volume

These are the musical terms and the abbreviations for volume. Other conventions use a mixture of French, German and Italian words in a variety of musical instructions. Young people may become confused when the word soft is used to mean quiet.

There is a strong tendency for volume levels to gradually increase throughout music sessions. Sometimes it is useful to call everyone to a stop and pull back the general level of work noise; however, making music is intrinsically a noisy pursuit. Gradual changes of volume are indicated by diverging or converging lines:

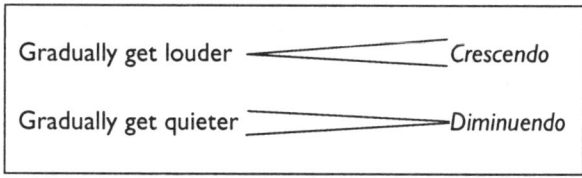

Changing Volume

Dynamics have a strong bearing on the intensity of music. At this stage we can equate quiet music with gentleness and intimacy, whilst loud music leads to feelings of boldness and vigour. A crescendo resembles music coming nearer, towards you, whilst the diminuendo represents going away, heading into the distance.

Volume is a further plate to 'spin in the air' as we continue on our musical journey. Each new ingredient becomes an additional companion for making music – timbre, pulse and now volume. So dynamics are another factor within every sound source and piece previously experienced. Is this instrument louder than that instrument? Will this drown out that? Does the piece begin quietly?

Continue to experience, discuss and invent using the ingredient of volume alongside timbre and pulse. This process will build strong musical concepts within our young people.

Rhythm

Rhythm work is reliant upon the foundation established in the beat/pulse work; it provides an exciting level of decorative intricacy superimposed over a steady beat. The walking beat/pulse used earlier can be viewed in a way which illustrates the important difference between pulse and rhythm:

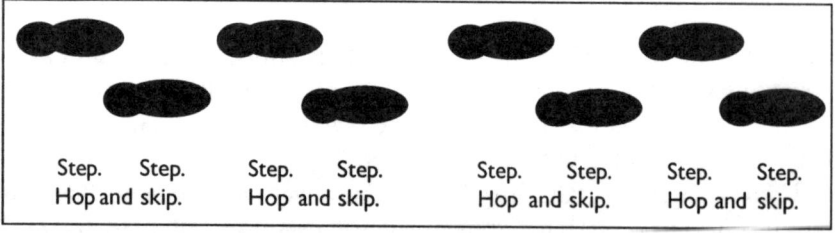

A Pulse and a Rhythm

Imagine that a child is hopping and skipping at the side of the walker. The walker strides out the beat whilst the child skips a rhythm. Try some rhythm playing based around any of the beats/pulses explored earlier. The rhythms can be freely improvised.

Perhaps your final composition is about a factory or machine.

- Set a beat going.
- Add other instruments to the beat. Improvise playing patterns which fit. Aim for repeating patterns if possible.
- Think about each instrument and its representation within the piece – a wheel, lever, ratchet or cog.
- Dynamics and timbre are also important considerations. A watch or clock may be quiet, using brightly toned instruments. A steel works machine would be a heavier composition, using a collection of loud, strident instruments.

The natural rhythm of words and phrases provide our next extension into the world of rhythm. They supply an interesting route to establishing repeated rhythmic patterns.

This is a machine piece based on repeating speech patterns:

Instrument	Speech pattern							
Sandpaper	Wash and	scrub.	Wash and	scrub.	Wash and	scrub the	whole day	long.
Wood block	Shirts,	socks,	vest and	pants.	Shirts,	socks,	vest and	pants.
Shaker	Bubbles from	soap suds,	bubbles from	soap suds,	bubbles from	soap suds,	bubbles from	soap suds.
Tambour	Wash	clothes.	Wash	clothes.	Wash	clothes.	Wash	clothes.

Our Washing Machine

Extend the composition by first saying the words, then words and instruments playing the rhythm of the words, following on with just instruments. Devise a signal to indicate when to change. This type of gradual build-up develops elementary ideas into longer compositions – variations on a theme. There is room for a mixture of freely improvised playing alongside the words and phrases.

A collection of words or phrases related to topics will inspire similar rhythm work. Here are some suggestions:

Growing in the garden
Things we like
This weeks weather
Countries of the world
Historical events

Food on the table
Types of transport
TV programmes
Book characters
Favourite sports

Develop your own themes and add them to your ideas book.

Pitch

Pitch is a simplified way of referring to frequency. In a scientific sense the human ear is receptive to frequencies from approximately 10Hz (cycles per second) to 20,000Hz depending on individual hearing ability; there is a gradual loss of the higher frequencies as we get older. Fortunately most musical instruments produce a range of frequencies lower than 10,000Hz. Every musical note produces a vibration – the faster the vibration, the higher the note. Tuned percussion instruments produce relatively high frequencies and used alone can technically deprive young people of the opportunity to handle truly bass sounds. There is also a disadvantage for those with hearing difficulties – often high frequencies are the most vulnerable to deterioration. The piano and electronic keyboard are the most common instruments that provide access to a wide frequency range.

Instrument	Range
Piano	(full range)
Bass Xylophone	
Alto Xylophone	
Soprano Xylo.	
Glockenspiel	
Soprano Voice	
Alto Voice	
Tenor Voice	
Bass Voice	

a b c d e f g a b c d e f g a b c d e f g a b c d e f g a b c d e f g a b c d e f g a b c d e f g a b c

middle c

55Hz   7,040Hz

Comparison of Pitch Ranges

This chart demonstrates our relative sense of pitch. (Playing a low note on a glockenspiel is completely different from playing a low note on the piano.)

Few people experience any difficulty in distinguishing between the lowest and highest note on a piano because there is such a large difference in frequencies. The human nervous system is good at recognising change. Initially strike wide contrasts when young people are establishing a sense of pitch. Confidence is enhanced when the individual clearly recognises the difference between two notes. Over a period of time gradually progress towards more exacting levels of pitch discrimination. The skill becomes more accurate with experience and repetition. Xylophones can be reared against a chair to highlight their physical orientation to high and low pitch, thus providing an extra perceptual clue for the player.

Sometimes people refer to music getting higher, when they actually mean louder. The absence of clear musical definitions quickly causes confusion. Some percussion instruments (such as xylophones, metallophones, glockenspiels, hand chimes and chime bars) produce specific pitches, whilst others such as drums, maracas and cymbals produce sounds of indeterminate pitch. These sets of instruments are described as tuned or un-tuned percussion.

Pitch readily equates with physical height. We can use this relationship to explore composition through contrast.

Pitch	Example 1	Example 2
High	Planets and stars	Mountains
Middle	The Earth	Moors
Low	Below the sea	Caves

Musical Contrasts

An example of content could look something like this:

Stars
- Select tuned instruments with the highest possible pitch. Play single notes in a steady way, 50 beats per minute. The notes could be a tune from the chime bars – **c♯, d, f♯, b**.
- Triangle, Indian bells and other un-tuned percussion playing in groups of threes and fours in clusters as directed.
- Continual gentle hits from a very soft beater on a large cymbal.

Earth
- A regular repeating rhythm played on a single 'Booming Bass' note **d**. (see Chapter 8).
- Low bass drum producing long rumbles.

Each piece plays in turn to provide the structure:

Earth – Stars – Earth

Composition related to gradual variation in pitch can be developed along these lines:

Pitch	Ex. 1	Ex. 2
High		
Middle	Flowing water	Roller-coaster
Low		

Gradual Pitch Changes

Flowing water
- Use approximately five tuned percussion instruments and gently glide the beater from the highest note to the lowest. Each instrument will be slightly out of synchronisation with the others.
- Shakers and maracas add directed pieces which start with fast shakes

and slow down over about ten seconds.
- Stroke across the piano strings throughout, fairly quietly [**mp**].

Roller-coaster
- A swannee whistle sliding up and down in response to the imaginary path of a roller-coaster. (Conducted or a line on paper.)
- Voices following a similar plan to the swannee whistle, using the sound 'Oooo!'
- A second group of voices providing squeals as directed.
- A football rattle gently rotated by hand (a ratchet sound).

All created music is an artistic interpretation, not an attempt to create a sound effect. These representations encapsulate mood and spirit in the same way small children may draw family portraits. Their mental imagery is likely to be more comprehensive than any immediate picture. Young people working on a roller-coaster piece may be recounting specific experiences. For instance, the football rattle sound indicated someone standing near the start of the ride, because they dare not take a ride. Additional information is always available by simply asking the composers to tell everyone about their composition before it is played. Talk is a vital part of this music making, particularly when contributions contain a high level of individual commitment.

Pitch compounds the overall musical complexity, thereby increasing the permutations between sound sources, timbre, pulse, dynamics, rhythm and volume. This is a long list. Young people need constant reminders and careful open-ended questioning to remember them all:

Have you thought about ...?
Try adding ...
What would happen if you ...?

Adopt strategies which provide the amount of help needed. This helps the young people to develop their own powers of thinking.

Form

This is the last of the musical ingredients to be examined in this chapter. Form is the plan or structure we give to the music. A simple plan is to link a series of musical events consecutively as represented in this diagram:

> A – B – C – D – E – F – G – H etc.

A simple order of different events

Repeats are a useful way of making the music longer:

| A – B – C – D – E – F – G – H | A – B – C – D – E – F – G – H |

Everything repeated

| A – A | – | B – B | – | C – C | – | D – D | – | E – E | – | F – F | – | G – G |

Each section repeated

For ease, convention uses capital letters for each musical idea. The string of events can be modified to have an idea which returns between the other ideas, the Rondo Form:

| A – B – A – C – A – D – A – E – A – F – A – G – A |

Rondo Form

A 'transport' rondo could be composed by having several groups working on their own mode of transport music:

Group B: Aeroplane music.
Group C: Boat music.
Group D: Car music.
Group E: Train music.

Between each piece everyone sings this song. Start on the note **c** and move one note lower for each half line. This song is the A section:

   c   **b**
| Trav – el the world by | land and sea,
    a   **g**
A | place in the sun is the | spot for me.
   f   **e**
With | tick – et to ride and | nev-er a care.
   d   **g** (make this **c** last time only)
So | pack your case, take | plen-ty to wear.

See Appendix 2 for a music version of this song.

Other useful forms to explore in your compositions are:

> A – B

Binary Form (Contrasts)

> A – B – A

Ternary Form

Plans for music making can be inspired by stories, poems and songs. The music will adopt their structures and themes. Characters, places, styles of movement, and actions are all available for musical interpretation.

Every conceivable instrument can be used in this type of work; orchestral, folk and classical instruments can play alongside tuned and untuned percussion instruments. Exploring all the ingredients of music is a fundamental activity and can become a life's work on its own. Continue to explore and experience the relationships between all the musical components to establish firm concepts of each. Maintain the compositions within a meaningful and descriptive musical context.

Listening

Expose young people to a diverse range of listening experiences. Seek out live performances whenever possible; listening to each other's compositions is an invaluable exercise. Tape record and listen to the performances of your own compositions, talk about, dance and move to music. A wide choice of recorded music is available. Look out for shops displaying low cost compilation tapes and compact discs. Offer an assortment of styles and idioms for our young listeners (see p.23).

Play a short example of the music with some indication of what to listen for – a particular feature, instrument, effect or event. There are many listening examples to illustrate variations in tonal quality, mood, rhythmic style, tempo, pitch: music telling stories, old music, new music and so on. The best choice of listening is related to activities and topics in other areas; establish relevant links and relationships wherever possible.

Begin a collection in your note book of suitable listening pieces; the radio, colleagues and friends are excellent sources. Be particularly aware of introducing stylistic breadth and include music from different cultures. Recorded listening requires factual information: the venue, the instruments, the way it is performed, the time it was first performed and

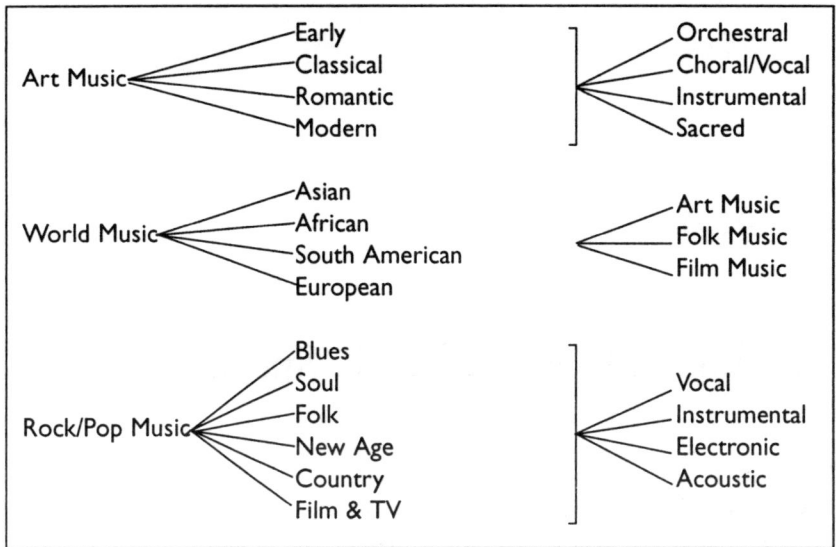

Types of Listening

so on, all detectable from aural clues. Keep notes of short musical extracts suitable for illustrating particular points.

Listening is pro-active. Note how our sense of hearing compares in a similar way to seeing; we can focus on sounds or block them out. We are also capable of scanning sound, adding things which are not actually there or using our memory and imagination to 'fill in' or fantasise. Focus listening efforts to combine the ear and mind.

CHAPTER 3

Moving on to Make Music Special

Many of the musical definitions in Chapter 2 were deliberately broad-based. The focus in this chapter becomes sharper, each area requires a higher degree of skill and the musical technicalities are refined, particularly in respect to rhythm and pitch. The structure remains constant: teaching of new content, followed by continual reflection of known musical ingredients.

Developing Pitch

It is essential to have a good stock of tuned percussion instruments within easy access. Xylophones, metallophones and glockenspiels are all useful visual instruments. (long bars = low pitch, short bars = high pitch). These visual relationships provide extra clues for discriminating pitch, as discussed earlier. With these instruments we are able to remove and change the position of notes. This is very helpful when working out the relationships between different notes, chords and scales.

Aspire to present a 'conversational' attitude toward playing music using different instruments. Conversation is spontaneous, easy and usually enjoyable. A pentatonic scale is effective for achieving this.

Pentatonic Scales

The pentatonic scale uses five different notes. Most classroom instruments present the notes twice over, helpful when two people are sharing.

Remove all notes **f** and **b**. Notice how the remaining notes fall into a pattern of 3's and 2's. There are many different pentatonic scales; a glance at the black keys on a keyboard instrument will reveal another (3's and 2's). Tuned percussion instruments have six pentatonic scales suitable for exploration.

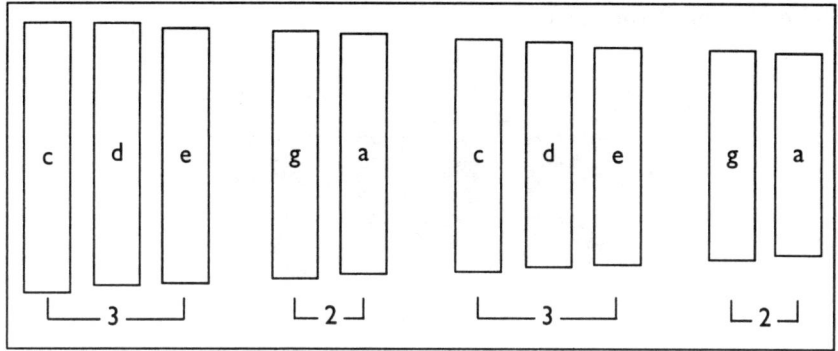

Pentatonic Scale Beginning on c

*	c d e	g a	remove notes f and b.
	d e f	a b	remove notes g and c.
	e f g	b c	remove notes a and d.
*	f g a	c d	remove notes b and e.
*	g a b	d e	remove notes c and f.
	a b c	e f	remove notes d and g.
	b c d	f g	not recommended.

* The most popular.

Pentatonic Scales

The pentatonic scales of **c**, **f** and **g** are the most popular These scales are musically 'safe' due to an inherent feature: no wrong notes are possible. Any number of players always sound melodious together. What a gift!

Try some walking music:

- Remove the notes **f** and **b**.
- Use an un-tuned instrument to set a steady walking beat.
- Invite tuned percussion to join in with any notes they choose from the pentatonic scale.
- Aim to have some of the players perform repeating patterns.

The musical distance between the notes in the scales marked (*) all create a concordant quality. Every individual contribution is perceivably pleasant; this is a valuable psychological tool for permitting the players immediate feelings of success. Scales 2, 3 and 6 possess a different flavour; they are more angular and discordant. Explore them after the other three; they are of particular interest for compositions requiring more edge. Add a description of their flavour in your notebook for future reference. Pentatonic scale 7 is not usable at this stage.

The Whole-Tone Scale

This six note scale is helpful when ethereal music is required.

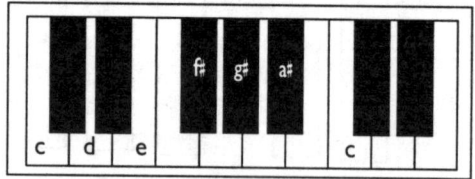

Whole-tone scale

Tuned percussion instruments require the additional bars of f♯ (sharp) and b♭ (flat). This is sufficient to provide the flavour of the whole-tone scale (without a g♯). Use the g♯'s if you have them.

A sharp raises, and a flat lowers, the pitch of the note by one semitone. The whole-tone scale naturally allows any note to fit with any other. Select the required notes and play away! The musical distance between each note of this scale is one whole tone, hence its name. This scale also has an automatic ability to sound good, irrespective of the notes played. Another musical gift for improvisation!

Technical Talk

The musical distance between notes requires consideration. The smallest musical distance we use is a semitone. Two semitones make one tone.

If we think of ascending a scale as climbing stairs, in semitones our staircase looks like this:

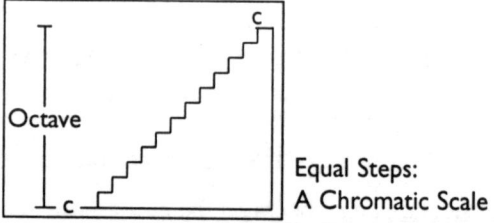

Equal Steps: A Chromatic Scale

Other scales have unequal steps to climb the same amount of musical height (octave). Examine the steps of a pentatonic scale:

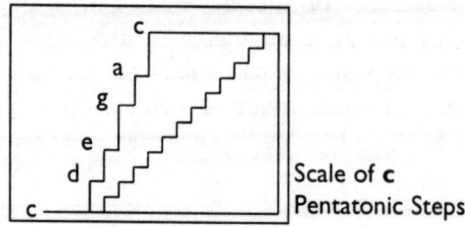

Scale of c Pentatonic Steps

Employing the analogy of ascending stairs is a useful way to explain pitch (higher and lower) in music. These diagrams are intended as background. The three-dimensional staircase design of chime bar holders or positioning tuned percussion instruments in a vertical plane, is additional information sometimes required by our young people. Further diagrams of major, minor and whole-tone scales can be found in Appendix I.

The logic of music has a number of inconsistencies in practice which do not immediately assist our understanding. Keyboard players establish a relationship between low pitch to the left and high pitch to the right. Guitars have strings positioned in the vertical plane; unfortunately the string nearest the ground is the highest pitched and vice versa. Piano accordions turn the keyboard into the correct plane yet, similarly to the guitar, the notes ascend higher as the player's hand nears the floor. Little wonder young people become confused. These instrumental anomalies should be identified.

Back to Scales

So, music uses a selection of notes to form scales, each possessing its own flavour or distinctive characteristic. A musical composition moves amongst different scales. Asian music uses Ragas, a collection of specific notes used in composition. They have characteristic flavours which are associated with spiritual themes. Ragas represent another series of scales to investigate.

Scales offer extensive opportunities for us to experience and explore through composition. Presenting a scale of notes and time to experiment is a good way forward. The scale is selected in relationship to the musical effect or mood required. Any scale represents a small portion of the complexities related to pitch. Experience inevitably plays a considerable role in making appropriate choices.

Strong Beats and Measures

We can build on the pulse work (Chapter 2) by examining the use of strong and weak beats. Imagine a spectacular Chinese dragon boat (a large canoe with ten or more paddlers). A drum plays out a steady beat to unite the paddlers. The drum is struck at the moment maximum 'pull' is required. It commands the crew to, 'Pull on the paddle!'

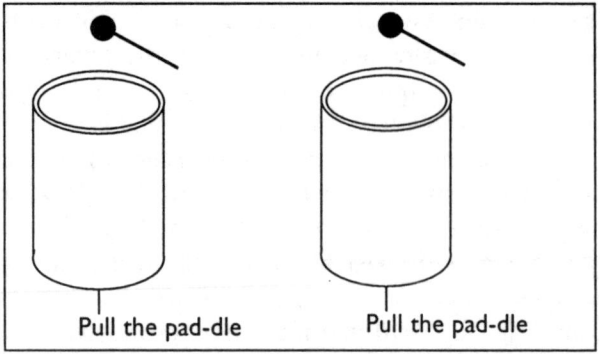

The drum is playing to mark the start of a cycle, a paddling cycle. The phrase constitutes a work chant, describing a synchronised activity. Music makes the first beat of any cycle stronger than the rest. The common cycles are measures of 2, 3, 4, 5, 6, 7, 8, 9 or 12 beats. The above example uses a cycle of 4 related to each word or syllable in this way:

> Pull the pad-dle
> 1   2   3   4

Regular Pulses with Accents

It is fun to play cyclic music, regular pulse music with different accents. Try a variety of patterns using percussion instruments, always accentuating the first beat (1). Become accustomed to playing and feeling the accented notes. (Strong accents are marked > in music.)

	>	>	>	>	>
A:	1 2	1 2	1 2	1 2	1 2
	>	>	>	>	>
B:	1 2 3	1 2 3	1 2 3	1 2 3	1 2 3
	> −	> −	> −	> −	> −
C:	1 2 3 4	1 2 3 4	1 2 3 4	1 2 3 4	1 2 3 4
	>	>	>	>	>
D:	1 2 3 4 5	1 2 3 4 5	1 2 3 4 5	1 2 3 4 5	1 2 3 4 5
	> −	> −	> −	> −	> −
E:	1 2 3 4 5 6	1 2 3 4 5 6	1 2 3 4 5 6	1 2 3 4 5 6	1 2 3 4 5 6

Accented Beats

Some of the regular pulses (C and E) have a strong beat in the middle (−), strong but not as strong as (>). If the middle accent was the same strength as the first, then all pulses would be multiples of two or three. Even the pulse of five (1 2 3 4 5) can be interpreted as:

```
          >   _       >   _
        | 1 2 3  1 2  or | 1 2  1 2 3
```

Avoid furious counting. Synchronise internal clocks by feeling the strong beats. Over-emphasising the accents is a helpful technique.

Musicians talk in terms of 'beats in a bar' when discussing the time element of music. The meaning and sense of dance music is related to strong beats, time and metre.

```
                   >
Waltz      |1 2 3|
                   >
Polka      |1 2|
                   >   >
Marching   |1 2|1 2| or
                   >   _
           |1 2 3 4 5 6|  (A strong beat for each foot)
```

African and Latin-American

African drumming employs very complex rhythm patterns based on a mixture of strong beats, time changes and the omission of beats (silence) from its cycle (those underlined).

```
A |1 2 3 4|1 2|1 2 3 4|1 2|

B |1 2 3|1 2|1 2 3|1 2|1 2|
```

Leaving out some of the beats is very complicated, particularly in example B. Notice how music is divided into bars by the use of a vertical line. The note after the line is always a strong beat. Using a musical convention such as bar lines helps to 'sow seeds' for later years.

Latin-American music sometimes employs this arrangement of strong beats:

```
    >      >     >
|1 2 3  1 2 3  1 2|
```

Work Suggestions

Playing accented pulses is a way of examining the underlying emphasis in music. Young people can enjoy the primeval experience of pulse and gain some understanding of musical measure before focusing entirely on rhythm.

Some ideas to further expand this topic are:

- Free improvisation based on different measures. Start with everyone playing the pulse then breaking out into free rhythm patterns whilst some players maintain the beat.
- Use signals to indicate dynamic changes.
- Add spoken or chanted words.
- Try echo clapping. The leader claps a short rhythm pattern and the rest of the group mirror it back.

Echo Clapping

A mixture of rhythms from the following phrases can be used as starting points for echo clapping. Establish a steady pulse and clap the rhythm of the words in time: add chanted words if you wish. Use this as a basic plan:

Breakfast Time

> We all eat our Cocoa Pops.
> Bacon and eggs are good to eat.
> Butter and toast on an old round plate.
> Sausage and mushrooms frying in a pan.

Each of the above phrases has a measure of 4; the important words fall on an accent. Exaggerate important words or syllables. Explore 3, 5 and other irregular metres.

Follow My Leader

Echo clapping extends into a 'follow my leader' idea to develop chanted words into singing. Imitating a singer can work in this way:

- First you require a simple tune, such as the beginning of 'Old McDonald Had a Farm'.

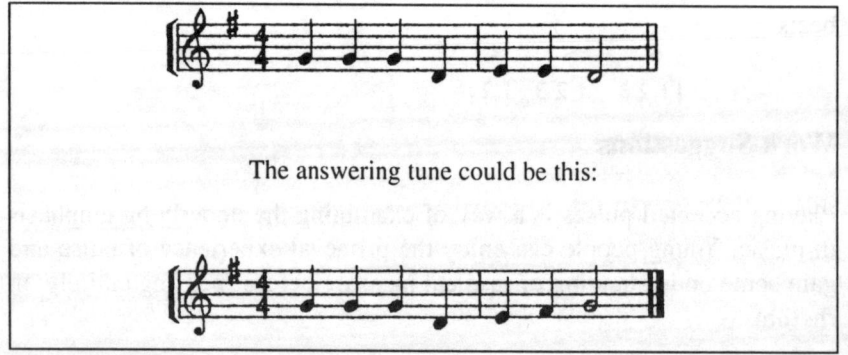

The answering tune could be this:

- Choose two rhyming words (e.g. spy, eye) then build up two phrases (ending in the two words) which also fit the tune.

   > I can see you with this eye,
   > Kalvinder and Freddie I can spy.

- Copy the two phrases in turn:

   > *Leader:* I can see you with this eye,
   > *Group:* We can see you with this eye,
   > *Leader:* Kalvinder * and Freddie* I can spy,
   > *Group:* Kalvinder and Freddie we can spy.

   * Use names of students in the group.

- Develop these two phrases using the same tune:

   > Claudette's coaches are the best.
   > Travel by bus and take a rest.

This example uses different words, a new tune (using two notes G and E) and a longer phrase.

> Peach-es, pears and plums
> Grand-ma chews them on her gums.

The rhythm can be adjusted to suit any words, keeping in mind the idea of working backward from rhyming words. This will help you to invent new examples to fit any particular topic or situation.

Early Notation

Throughout this book there are a number of references to becoming 'conversational' within the language of music. Although notation is secondary to playing music, there will always be times when ideas require recording in some way. The recording system used will inevitably reflect the level of sophistication required. Do not feel that traditional notation is an absolute system. A whole variety of marks on paper will serve young people until they are ready for increased complexity. Be warned, notation can easily take over from our main creative objectives.

As an introduction to relating ideas on paper to sound, try making a set of cards. You will need at least one card for each member of the group and the pictures should represent all the instruments available. Old catalogue pictures can be mounted on thick card. Repeat cards are required when you have more than one of any particular instrument. Try some of these ideas:

- Deal the cards. Young people find the instrument featured on their card. (This is a useful procedure to start a session.)
- Use several different colours of card as a method for sorting out different sub-groups (wood, metal, etc.).
- Select a number of cards from the pack, lay them out and play the instruments in that order. (Sequence.)

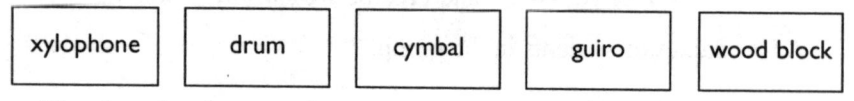

| xylophone | drum | cymbal | guiro | wood block |

- Here is a development for two sounds happening at the same time:

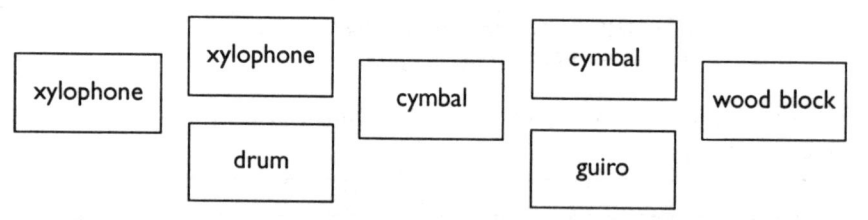

| xylophone | xylophone | cymbal | cymbal | wood block |
| | drum | | guiro | |

- Add blank cards to denote silence.
- Work out a specific musical event for each picture card. (Tune, rhythm, technique.)

Another notational technique is for young people to draw their own ideas on large sheets of paper, shapes to indicate the style of playing instruments. Your own ideas and those from young people are valuable; there are no set rules. The ideas are likely to include shapes and lines similar to these:

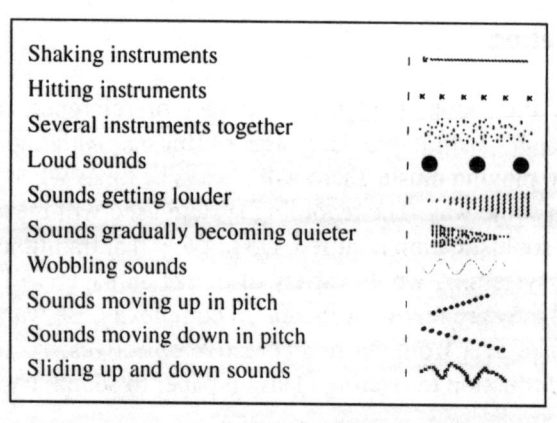

| Shaking instruments |
| Hitting instruments |
| Several instruments together |
| Loud sounds |
| Sounds getting louder |
| Sounds gradually becoming quieter |
| Wobbling sounds |
| Sounds moving up in pitch |
| Sounds moving down in pitch |
| Sliding up and down sounds |

Two conventions rapidly come into play when musical ideas are placed on paper. First, a left to right progression of events depicts the passage of time. Secondly, pitch is loosely related to the top and bottom of the page (high and low). A greater degree of sophistication is developed within the system by the use of regular vertical lines indicating the passage of time. A graphic score then has this flavour:

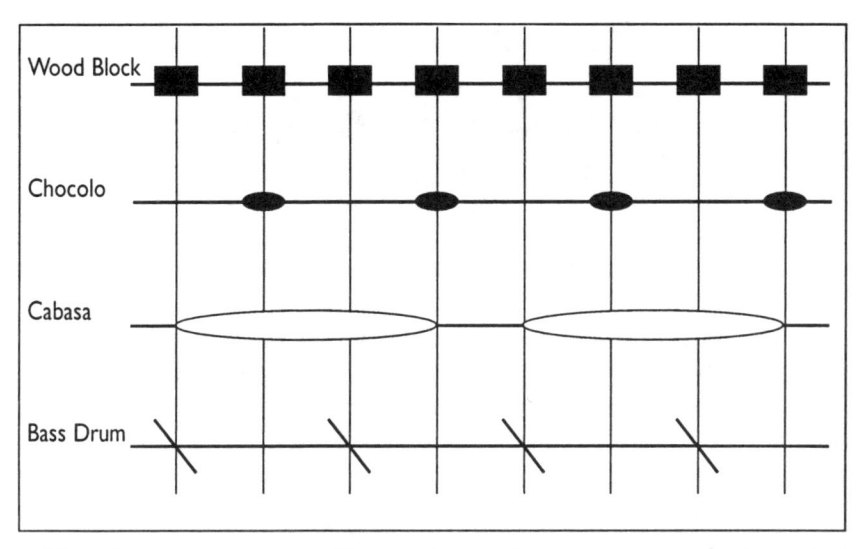

Notation systems generally require an immense amount of symbol drawing if the composition is of any length. The division of time into smaller units becomes crucial as a desire for more complexity emerges. Fortunately musicians will play music they cannot write down, in the same way that we say words we cannot spell. Reading out loud and writing are similar activities in some respects but the skills required are different. The same is true in music making.

Rhythm and Notation

The notation of rhythms can be established by initially focusing on a number of specific rhythm patterns related to speed. Depending upon the age and ability of your group, this is achieved by using a broad spectrum of symbols. Pictorial ideas through to conventional music notation can be employed. Word patterns and pictures provide a tangible link between rhythm, mind and paper. An illustration of these relationships could include a slow moving tortoise, boots stepping out in time, racing rabbits. These relate to slow, medium and fast movement. Speech patterns and notes are included in the diagram to assist in this visual, mental and aural association.

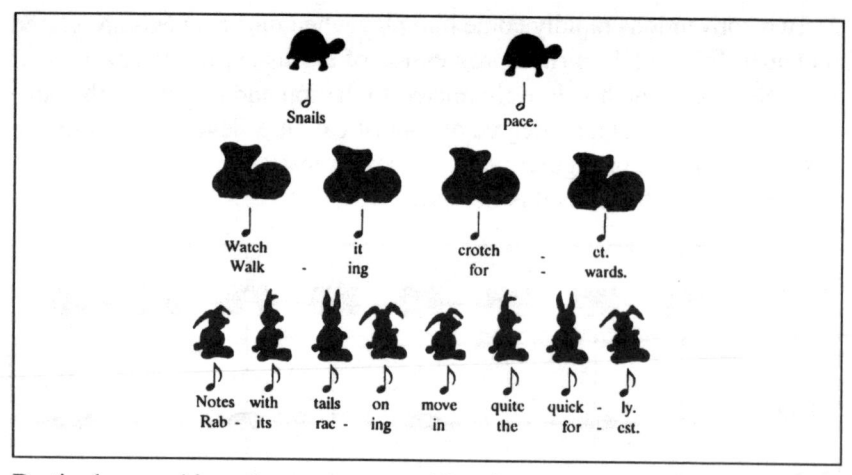

```
                    🐢                    🐢
                    ♩                     ♩
                  Snails                 pace.

          🐰        🐰        🐰        🐰
          ♩         ♩         ♩         ♩
         Watch      it      crotch       et.
         Walk  -   ing       for   -    wards.

     🐇   🐇   🐇   🐇   🐇   🐇   🐇   🐇
     ♪    ♪    ♪    ♪    ♪    ♪    ♪    ♪
    Notes with tails  on  move quite quick  - ly.
    Rab -  its  rac - ing  in   the  for  - est.
```

Particular teaching circumstances will reflect the time and relevance of when to use conventional notation. Remember, talking comes before reading. Our primary work is to build concepts of rhythm and pitch, to explore the relationship they have with each other and to imagine how the music will sound. It is very desirable for young people to be able to internalise – hear in their heads – their musical work. Notations are purely a way of assisting this process and the purpose of any symbol is to be mindful of sound.

Drones

Drones provide a simple form of accompaniment for melodies and are a useful addition to instrumental and vocal music. Drones are best described as notes continually playing throughout the music. Some instruments – such as bagpipes and the hurdy-gurdy – have drones built into their design. Bagpipes use three notes playing a continuous accompaniment on a drone whilst the tune is played on a pipe, the chanter. Tuned percussion instruments can be quickly set up for drone playing by removing all unnecessary notes and leaving the two required.

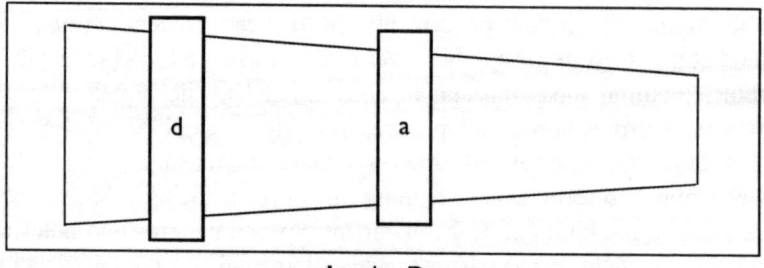

```
    ┌─────────────────────────────────────┐
    │        ┌──┐              ┌──┐       │
    │        │  │              │  │       │
    │        │d │              │a │       │
    │        │  │              │  │       │
    │        └──┘              └──┘       │
    └─────────────────────────────────────┘
```

d and **a** Drone

The two notes can be played together or alternately, whichever suits the feel of the music. Use a steady repeating rhythm for best effect.

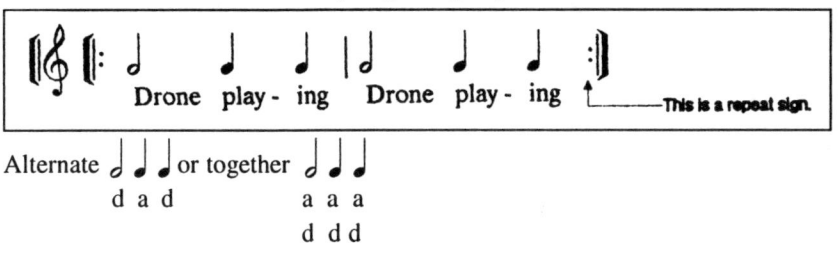

```
|𝄞 |: ♩    ♩   ♩ | ♩   ♩   ♩ :|
   Drone play-ing  Drone play-ing       — This is a repeat sign.
```

Alternate ♩ ♩ ♩ or together ♩ ♩ ♩
       d a d   a a a
                               d d d

Drone notes are a 5th apart (musical interval counting always includes the notes being played). The 5th is calculated by counting up the bars on the instrument from the lowest note of the drone through to the highest:

         d e f g a
         1 2 3 4 5

Use a drone, along with other instrumental parts, in a composition. Tuned percussion instruments require the removal of bars to leave the **d** and **a** drone, whilst other instruments need to be set for a pentatonic scale by removing notes **b** and **e**.

Pentatonic Scale f g a   c d
Drone   d   a

Use drone instruments to play a steady pulse and select smaller untuned percussion instruments for additional rhythmic accompaniment parts.

Decide upon the theme and consider using speech rhythms to help establish regular patterns. Build the piece by adding each part in turn.

A Walk in the Snow

Part 1   The Pulse. (Crunched newspaper)
Part 2   The Drone. (metal bars if possible) **d** and **a** to the rhythm of 'Snow and Frost'
Part 3   Rhythm Patterns. Approximately three at any time. Improvised.
Part 4a Pentatonic tune (metal bars **f g a c d**). Improvised initially, memorised or notated later.
Part 4b Pentatonic tune. An optional 'question and answer' game with 4a
Part 5   Vocal (using notes **f g a**) perhaps with a leader/follower idea (call and response):

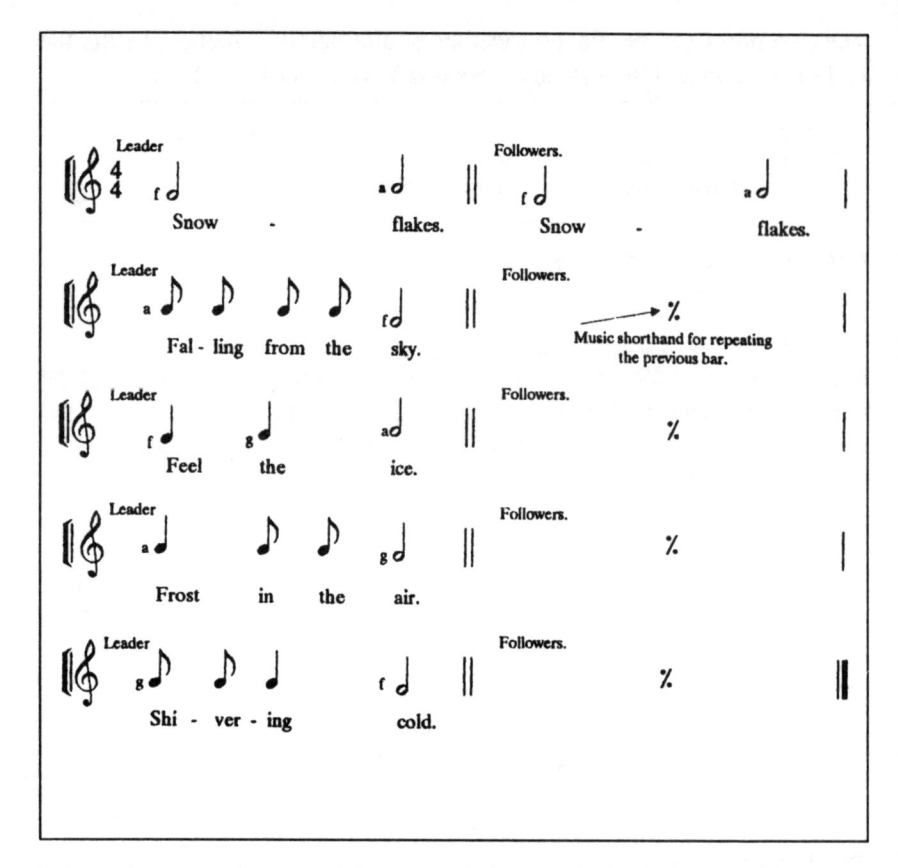

[Musical notation for a call-and-response piece with Leader and Followers parts:

Leader: "Snow - flakes." | Followers: "Snow - flakes."
Leader: "Fal - ling from the sky." | Followers: % (Music shorthand for repeating the previous bar.)
Leader: "Feel the ice." | Followers: %
Leader: "Frost in the air." | Followers: %
Leader: "Shi - ver - ing cold." | Followers: %]

Bring the piece to an end by reversing the build up: players gradually finish playing section by section.

When devising pieces of this nature, the pentatonic tunes can be improvised or structured, whilst words for singing could be self-written, selected from a story or poem, or derived from a textbook.

Expand the potential number of instruments available by including instruments the young people own. Here are some ideas:

- Cello, viola and violin all have the drone notes **d** and **a** on adjacent strings. Early players can be included after their first lesson.
- Recorders playing pentatonic tunes or drones, one player on each of the two notes.
- Keyboards/pianos can have notes which are not allowed (**b** and **e**) marked before they are used for pentatonic tune playing. (Re-usable adhesive putty makes good marking material.)

There are other drones available for use on xylophones, metallophones and other tuned instruments. Their notes are outlined here:

```
Drone notes
1  [c] d  e  f  [g]
2     [d] e  f  g  [a]
3        [e] f  g  a  [b]
4           [f] g  a  b  [c]
5              [g] a  b  c  [d]
6                 [a] b  c  d  [e]
7                    [b] c  d  e  [f#]
```

Drones

To present a wider choice of musical flavours, consider amalgamating some drones with pentatonic scales; by examining these relationships we reveal greater levels of musical complexity. Comparing the pentatonic scale notes with the drones, we discover these common factors:

Scale: c d e   g a   Drones: [c & g] [d & a] [g & d] [a & e]
Scale: d e f   a b   Drones: [d & a] [e & b] [a & e] [b & f]
Scale: e f g   b c   Drones: [e & b] [f & c] [b & f [c & g]
Scale: f g a   c d   Drones: [f & c] [g & d] [c & g] [d & a]
Scale: g a b   d e   Drones: [g & d] [a & e] [d & a] [e & b]
Scale: a b c   e f   Drones: [a & e] [b & d] [e & a] [f & c]
Scale: b not usable.

Pentatonic Scales/Drones

Spend plenty of time combining scales and drones within the context of your musical creations.

Tuned Accompaniments for Pentatonic Songs

Most pentatonic songs can be accompanied by using drones. Add more pentatonic melodies alongside the original tune. Here is an example using the drone **d** and **a** with the pentatonic scale of **f g a c d**.

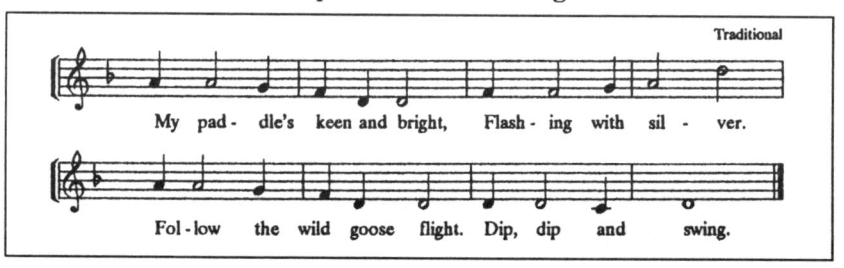

Traditional

My pad-dle's keen and bright, Flash-ing with sil-ver.
Fol-low the wild goose flight. Dip, dip and swing.

Following on, here is a further example of composition linking together a song with accompaniment for drone players. This piece describes a powerful army on the move into battle.

- The largest drum available plays the first beat of a regular pulse repeated throughout:

  ♩ ♩ ♩ ♩
  | 1 2 3 4 | 1 2 3 4 | 1 2 3 4 | 1 2 3 4

- A bright cymbal builds and releases tension by playing gradually louder and then gradually quieter:

cym

<> <>

- Add smaller drums such as side drums for soldiers marching:

  ♩ ♩ ♩ ♩
  Left, right, left, right . . .

- Add chain or other metallic clanks (sparingly), in time to the music to depict armour and weapons.
- Spoken voices gradually build up from a whisper, singing on one of the drone notes as you progress:

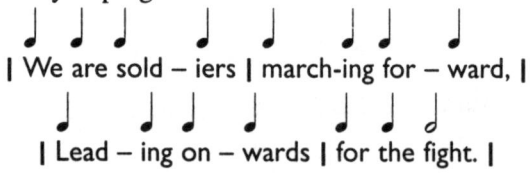

  ♩ ♩ ♩ ♩ ♩ ♩ ♩ ♩
  | We are sold – iers | march-ing for – ward, |
  ♩ ♩ ♩ ♩ ♩ ♩ ♩
  | Lead – ing on – wards | for the fight. |

- Then add drone notes [**e** & **b**] using the loudest and lowest instruments available (hard sticks for tuned percussion). The words below help the timing required:

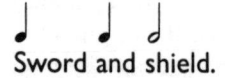

  ♩   ♩ ♩
  Sword and shield.

- Previously spoken voices change to singing their words using the lower of the two drone notes. The un-tuned percussion at the same time reduces its volume to an accompanying level. (Progress to using both drone notes for singing.)
- Singers stop.
- The instruments play on the **e** & **b** drone then change to a **d** & **a** drone according to this pattern:

```
b                b    b    b
e                e    e    e
Josh - ua fought the battle of Jer- i - co,

a      a    b    b
d      d    e    e
Jer- i - co, Jer - i - co.

b                b    b    b
e                e    e    e
Josh - ua fought the battle of Jer- i -co,

       a         a         b    b
       d         d         e    e
And the walls came tum - bl - ing down.
```

- You can add a jazz feel by incorporating Latin-American irregular pulses i.e. 123, 123, 12. Pianists can 'fill out' the drones with these chords on the piano:

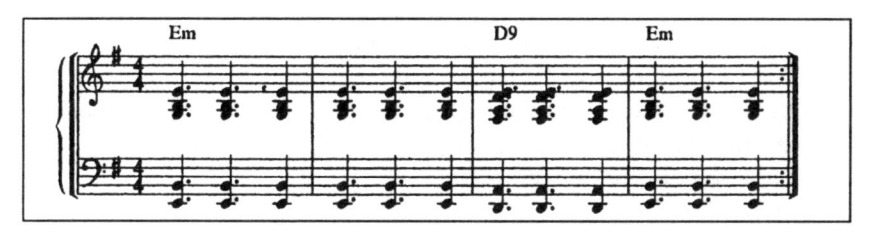

The **Em** chord relates to the **e** & **b** drone and the **D**^{9} chord complements **d** & **a**. The right hand notes are deliberately written low; it sounds better at this pitch. The rest of the song will fit to this same harmonic outline.

Ostinato/Ostinati

This musical term is used to describe a pattern repeated over and over. (Ostinati is the plural.) The technique is valuable because it allows players the security of repetition. Ostinati can be built one on top of the other resulting in quick and effective part work. The repeated ostinati patterns can be rhythmic, melodic or both. Other examples throughout the book make use of this technique.

Rhythmic Ostinati Compositions

A rhythmic ostinato could be performed with voices/un-tuned instruments or both:

[Musical notation with lyrics:]

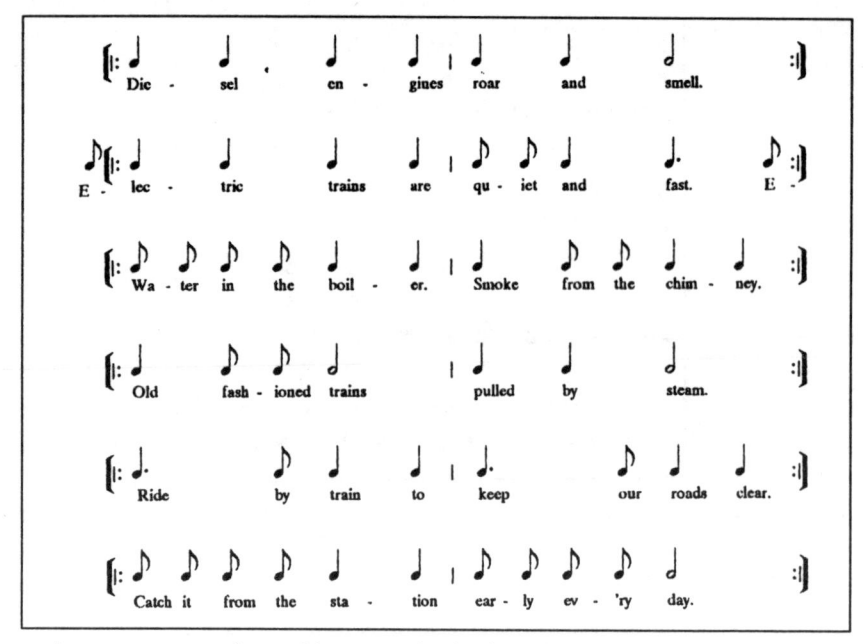

Die - sel en - gines roar and smell.

E - lec - tric trains are qu - iet and fast. E -

Wa - ter in the boil - er. Smoke from the chim - ney.

Old fash - ioned trains pulled by steam.

Ride by train to keep our roads clear.

Catch it from the sta - tion ear - ly ev - 'ry day.

As you can see from this example the length of patterns may vary and they can fit together at different starting points.

Pentatonic scales lend themselves to the composition of melodic ostinati. In the next musical example the pentatonic scale **c d e g a** is used to make a song from four short lines.

[Musical notation with lyrics:]

Trees are tall and di - gni - fied with

roots to hold them tight. Their

leaves reach out to touch the moon, And

ru - stle in the night.

'SFX' or 'Speed Music' is printed with a large typeface and has the letter names of the notes printed inside the note heads, similar to this example. It can be helpful in the early stages of working out note names. This music is readily available from most keyboard shops.

Add ostinati using tuned percussion instruments to accompany the singing:

Each bar and line of the original tune can also be used as ostinati.

Chord Playing

'Next-door-but-one neighbours' on tuned percussion instruments are notes which musically 'fit together' into pleasant chords. Although a variety of ways exist to build chords, the following description is the best for beginners. (These chords are also known as triads. They comprise three different notes which can be played one at a time, all together or in a broken pattern.) Chords could be considered as drones with a middle note added. Playing a chord 'all together' can be achieved by having a number of players joining in with the required notes at the same time. Progress to playing the chord alongside a pulse on un-tuned percussion.

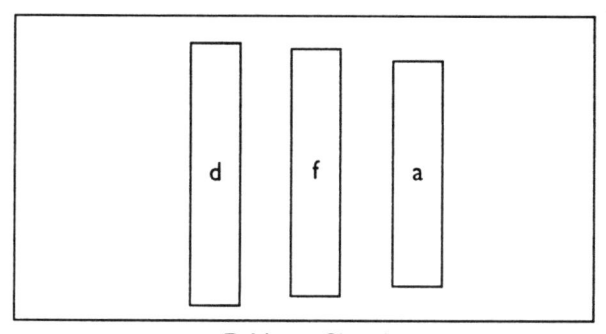

D Minor Chord

Play the notes **d f a**. Together they make a pleasant minor chord. Chords usually gain their name from the lowest note: **d** is the lowest note so this is the chord **D** minor. The chord is actually achieved by an overall sound of notes playing together. It is possible to have some players with only one or two notes from the chord. You can 'double up' notes in a 'mix and match' style to suit yourself. Here are the notes required for a number of chords:

I.	C major	c	e	g			C
II.	D minor	d	f	a			Dm
III.	E minor	e	g	b			Em
IV.	F major		f	a	c		F
V.	G major			g	b	d	G
VI.	A minor			a	c	e	Am
VII.	B diminished			b	d	f	Bdim.

The left hand note should be the lowest note played

Chords

See Appendix 3 for further information on the construction of chords.

Establishing Tunes Related to Chords

The notes of a chord and those contained in between them, provide a useful collection for making up tunes. Examining the chord of **D** minor presents the notes of **d f a**; the notes e and g are between the chord notes. Our useful collection of tune writing notes are therefore **d e f g** and **a**. Chord notes are the best for starting, ending and 'lingering on'. The other two notes (**e** and **g**) are for passing through along the way. Question and answer tunes can be developed using two players; the rest of the group can play the chord and/or rhythmic accompaniments.

Examine another chord – (**c e g**). These notes form the chord of **C** major. The in-between notes (**d** and **f**) combine to provide our collection for tune making. There is a very different 'feel' to this **C** major chord. Major and minor chords have different sounds because the musical distance between their notes varies.

Explore tune making with a limited collection of notes as described. It is also satisfying to play the chords for their own sake. Enjoy the musical flavours created from a choice of major and minor chords.

Playing Chord Changes

Begin by playing in groups. Have one group ready with the **D** minor chord and a second group prepared to play the **C** major chord. Start off by playing the **D** minor chord and then change to the **C** major chord at a given signal. After a period of time (8 or 16 beats) change back to the **D** minor chord. Carry on alternating in this way:

> D minor C major D minor C major

The conventional system for writing chords uses **m** to indicate minor. Unmarked chords are major. The shorthand form is:

> Dm C Dm C

Guitar players are very familiar with this shorthand system of identifying chords. Capital letters are printed for chords, lower case letters for names of individual notes **D = D major** chord. **Dm = D minor** chord, **d** = single note.

The duration of time spent on each chord is helped by acquiring a feeling of phrase. Play 16 pulse beats on each chord before changing to another chord. As confidence improves, chord changes can become more frequent, i.e. every 8 beats, every 4 beats or every 3 beats:

| Dm | / | / | C | / | / | Dm | / | / | C | / | / |

Song Accompaniment

The chords of **Dm** and **C** provide the building blocks for an accompaniment to the song 'What Shall We Do with a Drunken Sailor':

Dm
What shall we do with a drunken sailor,

C
What shall we do with a drunken sailor,

Dm
What shall we do with a drunken sailor,

C   **Dm**
Ear - ly in the morn - ing.

The last line has two shorter helpings of each chord, a not infrequent occurrence. This lack of consistency usually creates difficulties for early players.

The Link Between Pentatonic Scales and Chords

The diagram on p.25 illustrates the notes for a number of pentatonic scales. An examination of the chart reveals the potential for two different chords related to each scale. For example, the pentatonic scale beginning on the note **c** encompasses the chords of **C** and **Am**:

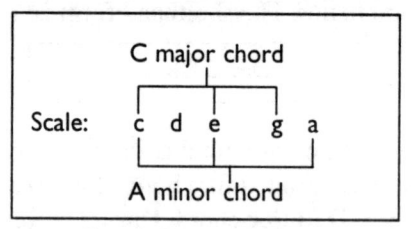

```
                C major chord
                    |
        Scale:  c  d  e  g  a
                   |     |
                A minor chord
```

Chords/Pentatonic Scales

All the pentatonic ideas can be extended by using the two available chords. You can work them out for other pentatonic scales when you require them. Write them in your notebook for future reference.

Take these ideas and develop them for your own needs and at a suitable pace. There is a great deal of information in this chapter. You'll need to revisit it as your work context changes and the young people develop musically.

CHAPTER 4

Increasing Sophistication

There are times when we need ideas to make music more appealing and plausible to those we work with. Electronic keyboards are designed to provide access, excitement and appeal. Some school music departments focus almost exclusively on electronic equipment because of its potential to make music credible and accessible to older pupils. Appeal is important to young people and electronic equipment is one of many solutions. We need ideas to establish and maintain a musical 'street credibility'. To engender feelings of, 'I want to do this!' closely followed by 'I can do this!'. These feelings are fundamental for positive achievement and personal progression for many young people.

This chapter is a kaleidoscope of thoughts, ideas, techniques and information to make music appealing to older individuals. Sophisticated ideas do have many instrument and resource implications; these require understanding over and beyond purely musical knowledge. Further developments in pitch, rhythm, timbre and so on are also included along with creative and technical concepts.

Instrument Stock

Begin by taking a careful look at your general stock of instruments and ask the following questions:

- Is there a good variety of instruments to choose from?
- Are they clean and attractive?
- Are they in a good state of repair?
- Do they produce intriguing sounds?
- Are they interesting to the young people?
- Is it time old and damaged instruments were replaced?

Make all instruments as attractive as possible. Teach how to take care of them, whilst avoiding an overly didactic approach as to how they should be played.

It is tempting to purchase cheap instruments in order to quickly accumulate sufficient resources to go round. A long-term purchasing plan is required to prevent this.

Beaters

Assemble a broad selection of beaters for achieving different tonal qualities. The beaters require differing sized heads made from wood, felt and an assortment of rubbers. The world awaits beaters which represent value for money! Avoid making do with any available stick.

Transducers: Extending Timbre

Transducers are to sound as a magnifying glass is to light. They are readily available from suppliers of electronic components. The transducer's main purpose is to act as a miniature loud speaker. (They are used in kitchen timers, clocks and other electronic gadgets.) In music we employ them to act as a very sensitive pick-up device, a magnifying glass for sound. The transducer works via an electronic amplifier. If you have access to Karaoke equipment or a music centre you can utilise their amplifier; the transducer will also plug into sockets used to amplify keyboards, a record deck, microphone or guitar. The device will require a length of cable and the addition of a suitable plug. (Bell wire works well.) The plug and wire will cost more money than the transducer. Buy several transducers. Bind them with sticky tape to prevent the electrical contacts breaking away. This is the wiring diagram:

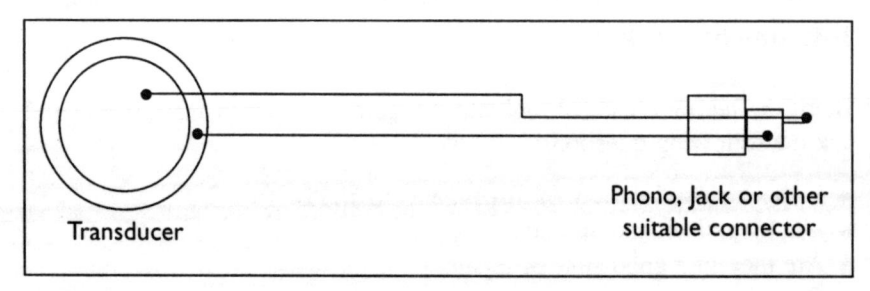

Transducer Wiring Diagram

Ask a friend or colleague to assist in wiring up, if you do not feel confident. There are five safety rules:

- Do not use old amplifiers with valves.
- Use transducers with equipment into which you would be happy to plug a microphone.
- If you are using water sounds, the amplifier must be battery operated.
- Follow the safety code set down by your place of work.
- Do not take risks.

These rules apply to transducers and all other electronic music equipment.

Once you have a transducer operational, begin to explore all the sounds, many of which normally go unheard. Hold or stick the transducer in direct contact with the following items. (Re-usable sticky putty is very useful for this purpose.) The amplified effects of a transducer can be stunning:

- Stretched rubber bands
- Different lengths of string, pulled tight and plucked
- A human hair, held tight and plucked
- Scissors, egg slicer, cheese grater and other household items
- Fix to a piece of thick cardboard. Stick pieces of differently textured material onto the card (sandpaper, leather, cotton wool, etc.). Stroke the different textures with your fingers.
- Fix to percussion instruments – gato drum, xylophone, metallophone, drum, guiro, maracas, etc.
- Hold a transducer onto the throat near the vocal chords and then explore vocal sounds.
- Fix the transducer to conventional instruments such as piano, guitar or violin.
- Make your own instrument and fix to the finished product. The transducer is guaranteed to add a new dimension to the most humble of creations.
- Use the sounds created to explore timbre, rhythmic and melodic ostinati, tune playing, etc.

Microphones and Recording

Many cassette recorders have built-in microphones to make recording quick and easy. Recording is a useful and immediate way of listening to your own compositions in an objective manner. Create a filing system so that you can find items at a later date. Tape counters vary from machine to machine; spoken descriptions recorded before the music are useful.

Two-Cassette Recording

Two recorders can provide an introduction to basic studio techniques. Start by recording a simple 'round' such as 'London's Burning' on one cassette. Whilst playing the recording back, sing the round again starting later. Record on the second cassette machine. This tape can then be played back whilst a third part is added, this in turn being recorded again, and so on. This is a crude way of multi-track recording; unfortunately the quality of sound is reduced on each recording. Purpose built mini studio cassette recorders are readily available and not too expensive. Multi-track recorders use a minimum of four independent tracks, with high quality results. (More multi-track ideas appear later in this chapter.)

Voices in Microphones

A microphone and amplifier provide opportunities for experimenting with vocal sounds. Using any form of voice amplification tends to disturb our self-perception, hence it quickly affects the way we react. All vocal sounds – spoken words, utterances and singing – are enhanced with amplification.

Echo Chamber

Echo chambers possess an engaging quality, and are easily added to a microphone and amplifier system. Contrary to its name the device is a small box of electronics, also known as digital delay units or effect processors. They create a different ambience and can be adjusted to imitate our voices in a cave, tunnel, cathedral or bathroom. Young people are often captivated by these enhancing effects which in turn inspire compositional ideas at many levels. The transducers, and other electronic instruments, (guitar, keyboard etc.), can be connected to an echo chamber. Music makes extensive use of echo effects either natural or electronic. They influence the overall feel of music and provide the opportunity to transport your compositions to imaginary locations.

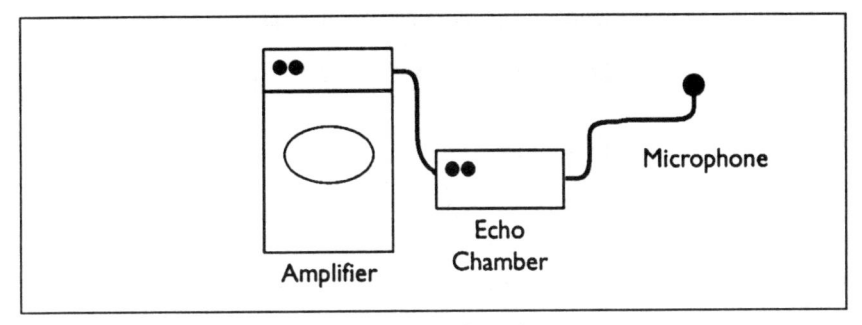

Wired for Sound

Riffs

Chapter 3 familiarised us with chord playing. Pop musicians play repeated chord patterns and call them riffs. Close to the end of Chapter 3 two chords were played alternately as a riff in this way:

Dm C Dm C repeated

Adjacent chords tend to work well together. Try this similar riff:

Am G Am G repeated

Add the two patterns together for a more complicated riff:

Dm C Dm C Am G Am G repeated

By including bar lines and oblique lines (indicating repeat beats of the chord) the music gains a slow three-beat feel and looks like this:

| **Dm** / / | **C** / / | **Dm** / / | **C** / / | **Am** / / | **G** / / | **Am** / / | **G** / / |

The rhythmic content is improvised around the chords.

Another way of writing the same piece would be to use roman numerals. (See diagram on p.42 for explanation of roman numerals.) This is another musical convention and may possibly be of benefit later on:

| **II** / / | **I** / / | **II** / / | **I** / / | **VI** / / | **V** / / | **VI** / / | **V** / / |

From Riff to Song

Known riff style chord patterns are often used by song writers. Rock musicians play the patterns over and over as instrumental riffs. A mixture of chords **I** and **V** are good for folk and country music. The pattern used for a song could be this:

A four beat feel with a steady amble.

|I / / / |I / / / |I / / / |V*/ / / |

|V / / / |V / / / |V / / / |I*/ / / |

Decide on a pair of rhyming words to fit at the marked points (*). Add other words to fit the musical measure. The words can be spoken above the chord playing. For example: tired old cowboy/pioneer style, perhaps with words like this:

> We | ride these plains the | whole day long,
> Our | great-est friend's the | mule.
> Through | blistering sun we | jour – ney on,
> 'Cause | des-ert's dry and | cruel.

Continue by writing a melody, achieved by using the 'notes within a chord technique' for the two chords of **C** and **G** (described in Chapter 3). We now have this:

```
      C  /  /  /   C  /  /  /   C  /  /  /  G / / /
   We | ride these plains the | whole day long, Our | great-est friend's the | mule.
Tune:
      g  c  c  c   d  e  e  e  f   g  g  g  e   g
```

```
      G  /  /  /   G  /  /  /   G  /  /  /  C / / /
   Through | blist'-ring sun we | jour – ney on, 'Cause | des-ert's dry and |    cruel.
      g  g  g  g   a  b  b  b   a  g  g  g  a    e
```

A simple way of making the tune longer is to repeat it. The second half of the song is a repeat, with a few slight changes at the end to provide a stronger finish. A music version:

The final arrangement of this song is enhanced by a guitar playing the chords, perhaps an instrumental verse (violin/recorder/glockenspiel) and some wood blocks for rhythm work to depict the clip clop of the mule's hoofs. Read on for an easy way to incorporate a guitar part.

'Bottle Neck' Guitar Playing

Guitar strings can be tuned in a variety of ways. This diagram shows a different tuning order. The open strings are tuned to become a chord of **C** major:

```
6th————————————note c
5th————————————note g
4th—————————————note e
3rd——————————————note g
2nd———————————————note c
1st————————————————note e
```

Bottle Neck Guitar Tuning

Use a keyboard instrument to match up the notes you require. Once the instrument is tuned, strum across the open strings to instantly play a chord of **C**. (The six strings are all tuned to notes **c e** or **g**.) Changing the chord is achieved by pressing down a small piece of copper pipe across all the strings in the appropriate place. Historically the neck of a bottle was used for playing the different chords, hence the name bottle neck guitar. Rock music shops sell a specific playing device (a small piece of chromium plated steel). The guitar can be positioned flat on a table and a few books placed under the neck to hold it firm during playing (Hawaiian guitar style). It is also possible to hold the guitar in a conventional position and use the index finger (perhaps the middle finger also) to press on the strings. Squeeze a small pencil rubber under any strings you do not like the sound of (perhaps the lowest **e** string). Use an electric guitar in the same way or add a transducer to acoustic models for a 'heavy metal' thrash.

Strumming and picking styles can be developed for song accompaniment playing, provided the song only requires major chords. These are particularly useful for rock and roll and the blues. The three important chords required are the open strings (**C** major) and **F** & **G** major. This diagram shows the finger positions for chords **F** and **G**. Hold all the strings down at the indicated places:

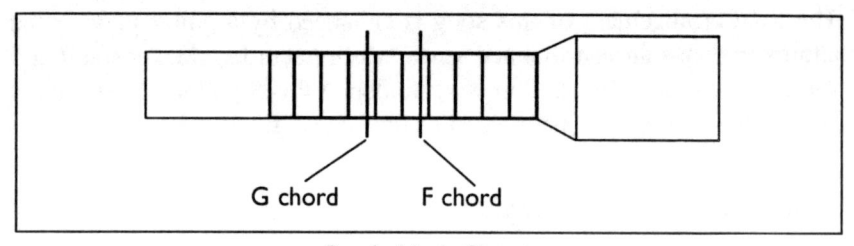

Bottle Neck Chords

More Riffs

Musicians enjoy a form of musical intoxication by repeating sequences over and over. We have covered two chord patterns. Here are a few with three or more chords in the sequence:

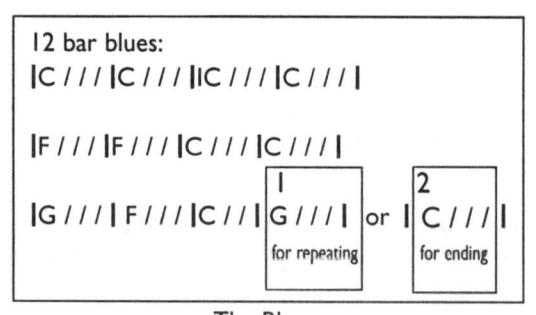

```
12 bar blues:
|C / / / |C / / / |C / / / |C / / / |

|F / / / |F / / / |C / / / |C / / / |

                              1            2
|G / / / |F / / / |C / / / |G / / / | or |C / / / |
                           for repeating   for ending
```

The Blues

Notice how the sequence has a first or second time bar at the end. Use the first time bar for repeating and the second time bar for the ending.

Riffs with Major and Minor Chords

When a piano lid is left open for any length of time a young person usually comes along and plays this sequence:

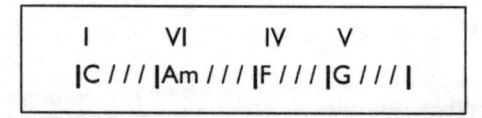

```
   I      VI     IV    V
|C / / |Am / / / |F / / / |G / / / |
```

The sequence often develops into a duet with an ancient pop tune played by a friend, over the top. Use this sequence in a wider sense. It has been a popular pattern since the time of Handel's *Water Music*. The 'Top 20' usually has at least one song written around this chord pattern, and always has had! The familiar nature of this sequence naturally leads into other familiar chord patterns employing a mixture of major and minor chords. Major and minor chords are described in Appendix 3.

This is a slight variation from the previous example:

```
 I      III    IV     V
|C / / / |Em / / / |F / / / |G / / / |
```

And more favourites to try:

```
 III     VI    III    VI
|Em / / / |Am / / / |Em / / / |Am / / / |  (a middle section)

 IV      V     IV     V
|F / / / |G / / / |F / / / |G / / / |  (a middle section)

 I       II    III    IV
|C / / / |Dm / / / |Em / / / |F / / / |
```

Some of these sequences may be combined with earlier riffs to provide beginning, middle and end sections.

This example combines sequences to construct an A-A-B-A-A song plan:

	I VI VI V
First section **(A)**	|C / / / |Am / / / |F / / / |G / / / |
	I VI VI V
Repeated	|C / / / |Am / / / |F / / / |G / / / |
	IV V IV V
Middle section **(B)**	|F / / / |G / / / |F / / / |G / / / |
	I VI VI V
First section again **(A)**	|C / / / |Am / / / |F / / / |G / / / |
	I VI VI V
	|C / / / |Am / / / |F / / / |G / / / |
	I
	Ending. |C / / / |

A Song Outline

Explore these two sequences to formulate another song plan:

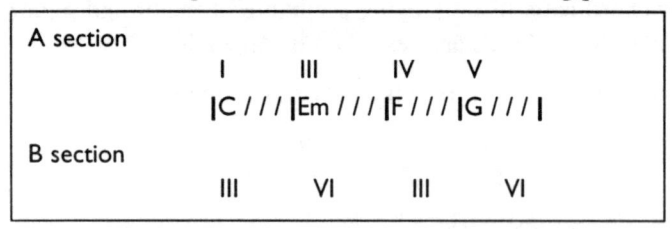

A section				
	I	III	IV	V
	|C / / / |Em / / / |F / / / |G / / /				
B section				
	III	VI	III	VI

The chords I, IV and V are the most fundamental of all harmonies because many tunes can be accompanied using just these three chords. Every note of a major scale is common to at least one of the chords, as this illustrates:

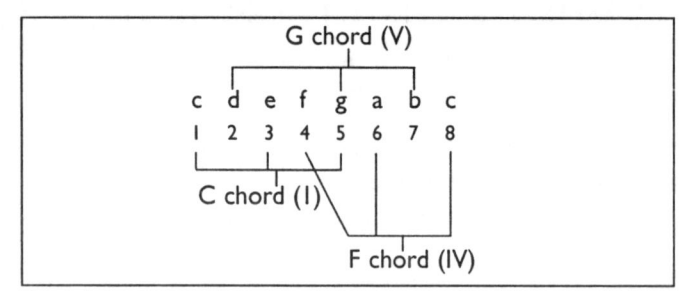

```
            G chord (V)
         ┌─────┬─────┐
    c  d  e  f  g  a  b  c
    1  2  3  4  5  6  7  8
    └─────┬─────┘
      C chord (I)
                   │  │  │
                F chord (IV)
```

Chords/Scales

If you consider the notes 'inside' the chord notes (known as passing notes) along with the above information, you can teach young people how to make informed choices about which chord to place where in a tune. This matching up process between tune notes and chord notes forms the basis of harmony.

Conventional Notation: Time, Metre and Rhythm

Music notation is proportional in design. Notes are accurately placed on the page to give a visual clue as to the pitch and duration of each note. We are basically looking at a graph plotting pitch against time. Unfortunately, there are a number of secret codes to be deciphered. The next few paragraphs will help in decoding the process.

The first code we meet on a line of music is a 𝄞 treble clef (a fancy letter **g**). After the clef comes the time signature. Time signatures are the code for where strong beats are going to land. If we examine 2, 3 and 4 beat music the time signatures will be:

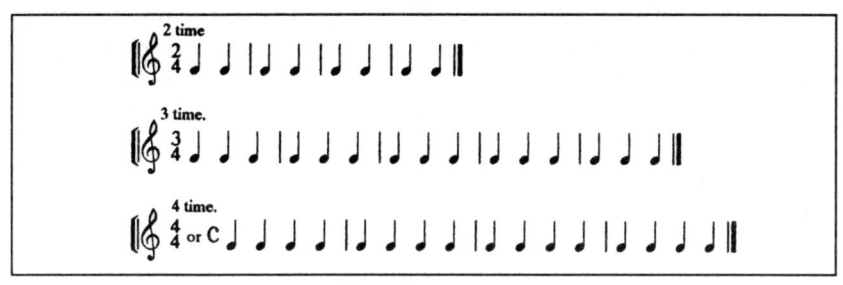

Time Signatures

Time signatures have two digits. The top number relates to how many beats and the lower to what size. There are only three 'what size' numbers to remember:

2 = minims (half notes),
4 = crotchets (quarter notes),
8 = quavers (eighth notes).

Simple mathematics is used to make all the notes in each bar add up. Notes can be of any value provided the bar does not 'bust'.

Americans use a system for naming notes which is helpful when interpreting time signature codes. It has a relationship with the lower figure in time signatures and goes like this:

English Name	Note	American Name
Semibreve	o	Whole note $1/1$
Minim	♩	Half note $1/2$
Crotchet	♩	Quarter notes $1/4$
Quaver	♪	Eighth notes $1/8$

Clearly the logic for the American names is derived from a simple division of the whole note into half-notes, quarter-notes and so on. Each note also has a time length which is related to the pulse/beat of the music:

o = 4 beats   ♩ = 2 beats   ♩ = 1 beat   ♪ = $1/2$ beat

Rhythm is represented by using an assortment of note values. It is important to allow the rhythmic ideas to come first and the writing down afterwards. Many musicians become versed in their art without feeling any need to write down their music. Possessing the rhythmic ideas and allowing them to flow are the most important. If you compare notation in music to reading and writing skills, it is clear how restrictive conversation would become if every convention demanded technical accuracy on paper. Speech patterns, described earlier, are extremely useful in assisting our eyes and ears to recognise stock rhythm patterns. These are examples with a thematic approach – review them by inserting your own subject material:

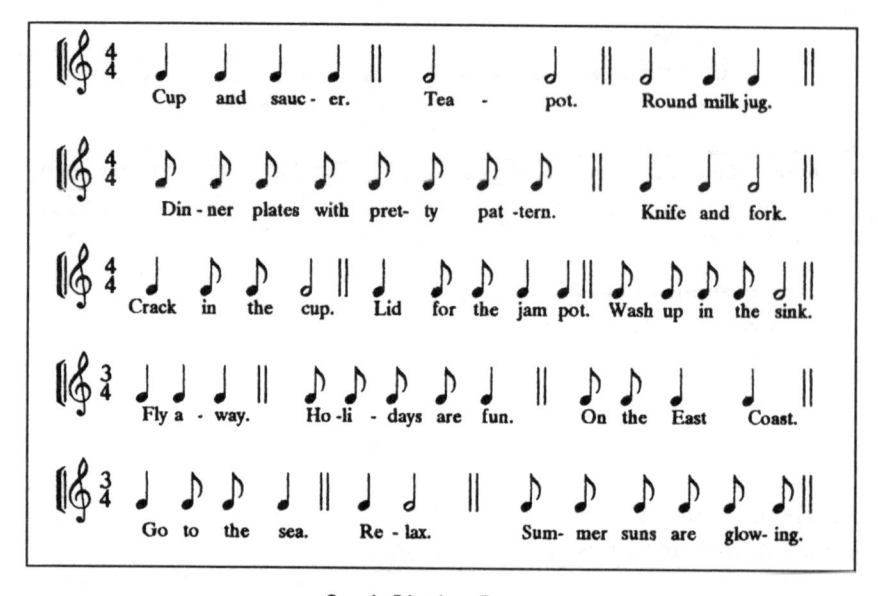

Stock Rhythm Patterns

Speech patterns related to the experiences of young people have the greatest significance.

Four more theoretical points complete the picture:

- Notes can have a dot placed after them. This increases the note value by half its original length: 𝅗𝅭 = 3 beats, ♩. = 1½ beats and so on.
- Sometimes notes of less than one beat are grouped together: ♫ ♬
- Notes can be inverted: ♩ ♩ ♩
- Notes on or above the middle stave line have their stems down; those on or below have their stems up.

Conventional Notation – Pitch

The system for the notation of pitch is absolute and thus is less complex on paper. We have discussed plotting the relationship of time against pitch in a graphical way. Building up five lines of a musical stave is a way of making the graph more specific. The system works like this:

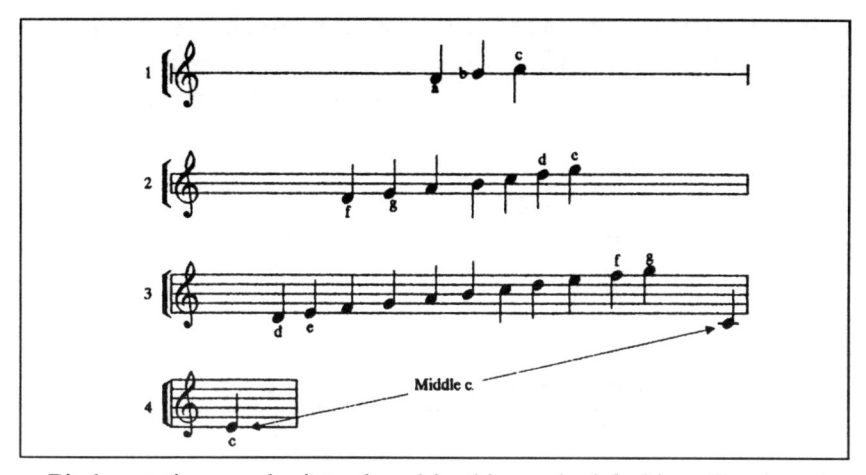

Pitch notation can be introduced in this gradual fashion. Continue by adding lines and spaces; in fact music does that beyond the usual five lines by employing a small portion of line when necessary. Note how the middle C requires a line drawing. Without such a system music would be even more confusing. (See the next example.) Use several techniques for teaching the reading of music. These include a line at a time, letter names over the notes, use of different colours for notes, and so on. Individuals respond to varied approaches. There are many valuable ways of introducing the topic of pitch; all require firm roots in practical music making to be of any great value. Flexibility of approach is important due to the perceptual inconsistencies inherent in the system. For example, piano music plays tricks on visual perception – the space between the staves is 'opened up' implying a space greater than the actual three notes:

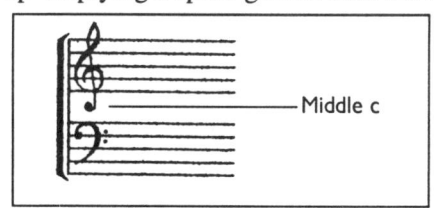

D, F and G Major Scales

Because pentatonic scales and the whole-tone scale tend to be less complex, they are preferred in the early stages of improvising music. Major scales demand a more general understanding of scales (typified by *Doh, ray, me, fah, soh, lah, te, doh.* Tonic Sol-fa). Appendix I illustrates the musical distance between the seven different notes of these scales.

It is possible to start on any note of a glockenspiel and work out the notes of a major scale. Additional sharps and flats will be required – the equivalent of black keys on a keyboard. Most new classroom percussion instruments arrive with the extra notes of f♯ (sharp), b♭ (flat) and c♯ (sharp). With these three additional notes the following major scales are available:

G major.

F major.

D major.

Major Scales

The major scale from **c** to **c** naturally occurs on the instruments without the need for any sharps or flats.

Sharps and Flats

Sharps and flats are required to provide every note with a name. A note which is a semitone higher is sharpened (♯) and a note which is a semitone lower is flattened (♭). Using this information, observe how all black notes on a keyboard have two names. There are rules, depending on a number of circumstances, to decide which name should be used. Refer to a music theory book if you require this information. The whole point of the flats and sharps is to allow tunes to be played higher or lower to correspond with the 'range' of notes available to singers or instruments. For example, the scale of **d** is a little higher than the scale of **c**; the scale of **f** is much higher. Tunes and chord sequences can be transposed to different scales. (Hence the earlier use of roman numerals which become universally applicable to any scale.)

Key Signatures

Music notation adopts key signatures to avoid writing sharps or flats before every note requiring them. The convention is to write them once at the beginning of each new line:

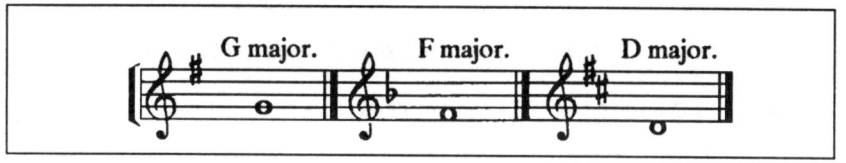

Key Signatures (G major. F major. D major.)

With many things to think about when playing music, sharps and flats written at the beginning of a line can easily be forgotten. If this becomes a problem write them in as required. Use a soft pencil so that they can be rubbed out later when you are familiar with the tune.

Aeolian and Dorian Modes

Modes are the historical forerunners of major and minor scales (pre-1600). They are easy to use, have a distinctive musical flavour and remain in evidence through the music of today. The Dorian mode is a particular favourite of mine. The notes of this mode are easy to remember because they are the 'white notes' only from **d** to **d** (remember **d** for Dorian). The white notes on a keyboard from **a** to **a** present another mode which is useful for tune playing, again easy to remember (**a** for Aeolian). Modes are types of scale which lend themselves to melodic improvisation. Try out the Aeolian mode with an **a** drone or an **a** minor chord as an accompaniment. The instrumentation, speed, pulse, metre and rhythm should be related to the mood you wish to create. Remember the importance of each component. Jazz and rock musicians make extensive use of these two modes for improvisation work.

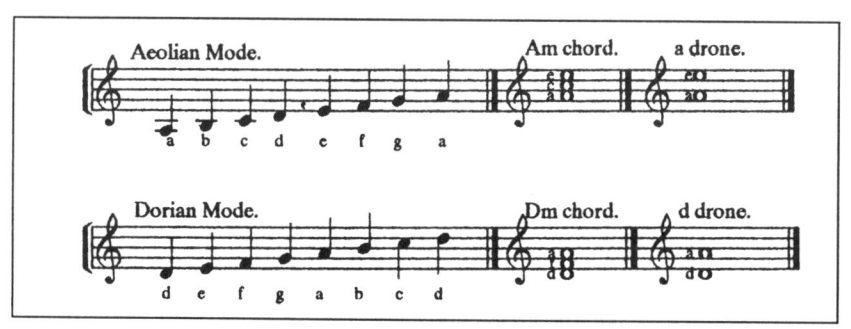

Related Drones, Chords and Modes

Once you are familiar with the modes, experiment by changing from one to the other: start on the Aeolian for 8 bars, then change to the Dorian for another 8 bars and keep alternating. The chord and/or drone will require changing in line:

```
| Am / / / | Am / / / | Am / / / | Am / / / | Am / / / | Am / / / | Am / / / | Am / / / |
| Dm / / / | Dm / / / | Dm / / / | Dm / / / | Dm / / / | Dm / / / | Dm / / / | Dm / / / |
```

Additional chord/drone changes could be incorporated for increased complexity:

```
Aeolian –    |Am / G / |F / G / |Am / G / |F / G / |

Dorian –     |Dm / Em |F / Em |Dm / Em |F / Em |
```

Notice how there are two chords for each bar.

Many playing references have been made to tuned and un-tuned percussion instruments. Many orchestral and folk instruments can also be used to play effective tunes and accompaniments. During their early musical experience, instrumentalists should be encouraged to experiment with pentatonic scales, whole-tone scales, modes and chord playing as a matter of course.

Transposing Instruments

Some instruments require music to be transposed before their playing will fit alongside concert pitch instruments. A little knowledge is required to accomplish this. If the player reads a note on a concert pitched instrument, then plays it, the read note and the heard note will be the same. (Read note **a**, sound note **a**). Concert pitched instruments include:

Xylophone	Glockenspiel	Metallophone
Chime Bars	Hand Chimes	Recorder
Flute	Oboe	Bassoon
Trombone	Violin	Viola
Cello	Double Bass	Keyboards
Descant Recorder	Guitar	Mouth Organ

Instruments of Concert Pitch

All the above instruments can happily become involved in all the playing examples in this book, exactly as they appear on the page. Transposing instruments has developed to make things easier for the player, often to help with fingering. To make things work out musically the clarinet, trumpet, cornet, tenor saxophone (and any other instrument referred to as a B♭ instrument) will require every note to be played one tone higher. To hear the note **c** the player will read the note **d**. A chart to assist with this process appears at the end of Chapter 7. All saxophones and most brass instruments are transposing instruments; some of them have different degrees of transposition.

Electronic Keyboards

Keyboards are rather like cars, they all have the same basic controls but every manufacturer changes the layout for each individual model. Small keyboards (like any computer) are designed for one player to operate. One or two keyboards can be effectively employed in group situations. However, it is extremely difficult to work productively with large numbers of similar sounding instruments. The following description examines the general aspects of all keyboards. How you access each function will require reading the instruction manual, or trial and error.

Keyboard Voices

A button-pushing routine will quickly allow the exploration of an expansive range of voice sounds. An average keyboard will contain 100 different sounds including drums, electronic, special effects and instrumental voices. Some sounds will play for as long as a key is held down (organ/string) whilst others will decay after a period of time (piano, harpsichord). This array of sounds can greatly extend the range of instruments available in a composition. The keyboard may be used as a sound source for all the timbre and rhythm work covered earlier.

Keyboard Styles

Percussion instruments are grouped into drum patterns for a variety of rhythmic styles – tango, rock, ballad, waltz, etc. The speed can be adjusted. Try using the styles for accompanying echo clapping: listening is the secret of good time keeping. Be aware of styles which are too busy for young ears. If the design incorporates variations on the same rhythm pattern, use the least cluttered.

Keyboard Chord Accompaniments

Most keyboards can be used to play an accompaniment using only one finger. Different manufacturers call this feature by their own name (ABC, Single Finger, Wonder Chord, etc.). If the keyboard has this feature it will definitely operate over the bottom octave of keys:

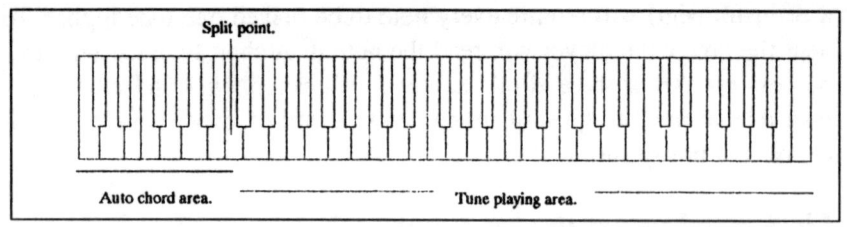

[Keyboard diagram: Split point. Auto chord area. Tune playing area.]

More sophisticated keyboards have the ability to choose a split point higher up the keyboard. Notes to the right of the split play voice sounds.

The following is a basic note required to start a keyboard accompaniment. Every keyboard piece should be preceded by this sequence of events. Prepare to play by programming the style and speed into the instrument:

1. Select a suitable style (rap, rock shuffle or funk)
2. Set the speed you require (110)
3. Press Syncrostart (if available on your keyboard)
4. Use your left hand index finger as if pointing. (Not very pianistic in style but the most functional for operating these instruments). Press the key corresponding to the chord note written above the music.

An accompaniment for a rap can be achieved in minutes. Use the style and speed information already programmed. Press the note **g** in the auto chord area and rhythmically recite the following words. Observe where the chords change:

Chorus
|G|
Rapping along.
Rapping along.
Everyone shout,
We're rapping along.

Repeat.

Verse
|G|
Rapping is the style for me,
|B♭|
As simple as your A B C.
|C|
The crowd all know I'm in the groove,
|G|
Feel the beat, get ready to move.

Repeat Chorus

A keyboard works out the drum pattern from the one (single) note, along with bass lines and chordal accompaniment. Local keyboard shops will have a wide selection of music written out for keyboards in a suitable format. Sheet music has chord letters written in the music; they are also found in children's song books. Use a highlighter pen to make the chords stand out. Search out some music and experiment with these techniques. There are other ideas related to keyboards in Chapter 7.

Two further technicalities require clarification:

- Chords with numbers **D7, G9, Csus 4**, etc. Ignore the numbers at this stage. Play the basic chord. (**D, G, C.** etc.)
- Chords with lower case m's – **Am, Em**. The lower case represents a minor chord. Single finger chord systems require more than one note to be pressed at the same time to achieve minor chords. Systems vary with the manufacturer. Yamah uses any black key to the left of the chord note. For a chord of Am this would be:

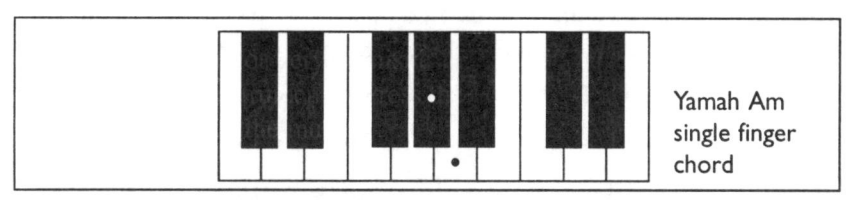

[keyboard diagram]	Yamah Am single finger chord

Check the instruction manual for other makes. All models from the same manufacturer employ the same system.

Hi-tech Equipment

Technology moves at a rapid pace and computerised musical equipment is extensively available. High-tech musical equipment is extremely fashionable with young people. It is extensively portrayed in the media and influences many of the popular musical models of today. Chart material makes extensive use of autochord keyboard facilities similar to those already examined. Here are some further high-tech avenues to explore.

Multi-Track Recording

A crude, low cost way of multi-track recording is described on p.48. Purpose built multi-track recorders are available from hi-tech music shops; they become less expensive as time goes by. These machines use standard audio cassette or newer digital formats and have great potential. They provide an adequate introduction to the principles of tracking – recording music and then adding more music in stages. Ensure the first track is accurate and to your satisfaction, before moving on to record the others. All events sound as though they were happening at the same time when the tape is played. Only those who made the recording know the time elapsed between each musical event. Inevitably the instruction manual for each individual recording machine is essential for finding your way around. Tracking allows musical events to be recorded at differing times in a synchronised way. The finished tape sounds as if the individual strands of the performance are happening simultaneously.

Plug a microphone into Track 1 of the machine and try this simple rhythmic exercise:

Multitrack Rhythmic Voice Piece

Record the following words making each represent a percussion instrument. Rehearse the sounds first: make all the sounds with your mouth, adjusting the tone and pitch accordingly:

Bass Drum.	Boom / Boom /	Boom / Boom /	etc.
Maracas.	Tsss Tsss Tsss Tsss	Tsss Tsss Tsss Tsss	etc.
Cymbal.	Pchsssssssssssssssssss	Pchsssssssssssssssssss	etc.

- Set the machine to record Track 1
- Sing the bass drum part many times – say, one minute's worth.
- Listen to the recording. If it is satisfactory then move on. If it is unsatisfactory, record again.
- Set the machine to record Track 2 and play Track 1.
- Sing the maracas part along with the bass drum.
- Listen to the two parts together and move on if you are satisfied.
- Set the machine to record Track 3 and play back Tracks 1 and 2.
- Sing the cymbal part along with the other tracks.
- Listen to the three parts together and then record the final track.

Multitrack Instrumental Piece

Track 1. Set to record. Use the rhythm unit from a keyboard. Start with a disco style at approximately 120 beats per minute. Gradually turn up the volume to make the rhythm fade in. After several minutes fade out the rhythm.

Track 2. Listen to the rhythm on Track 1 and then add some chords. On a tuned percussion instrument try:

| o | o | o | o |
| Am / / / | Am / / / | G / / / | G / / / | etc.

Continue playing until the rhythm stops. Tidy up the ending later.

Track 3. Add a simple two-note part to provide harmonic complexity:

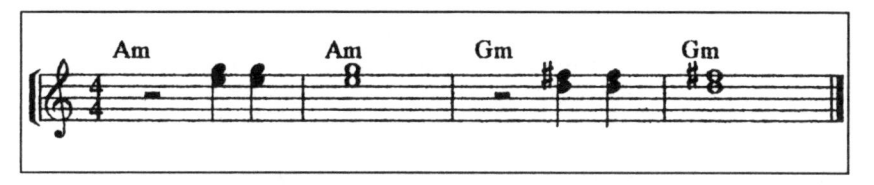

```
    Am        Am        Gm        Gm
```

Track 4. Add a tune on a recorder, flute, clarinet or tuned percussion, based around the notes **c** and **d**. (Improvise your own.)

An ending for the piece is achieved by slowly moving the main volume control down, resulting in a gradual fade out (in line with the dynamics of Track 1). Fade outs are often used in pop music as a convenient way to end a piece.

Tracking forms an essential ingredient for most recorded music. The technique creates an illusion of time travel in the overall effect of the finished product. There are occasions when orchestras play an accompaniment using tracking techniques and add a soloist at a later date – perhaps in a different part of the world. The information recorded on a multi-track machine will have to be copied onto a standard cassette recorder for general listening.

Midi

Midi is an acronym for **M**usical **I**nstrument **D**igital **I**nterface. It is the universal standard, allowing pieces of electronic musical equipment to communicate with each other. Midi can be immensely complex, but, it also has some simple aspects we can readily use.

Linking Two Keyboards Together With Midi.

Two keyboards with Midi connections could be connected together in this way. Midi leads are readily available from electrical and hi-tech music shops:

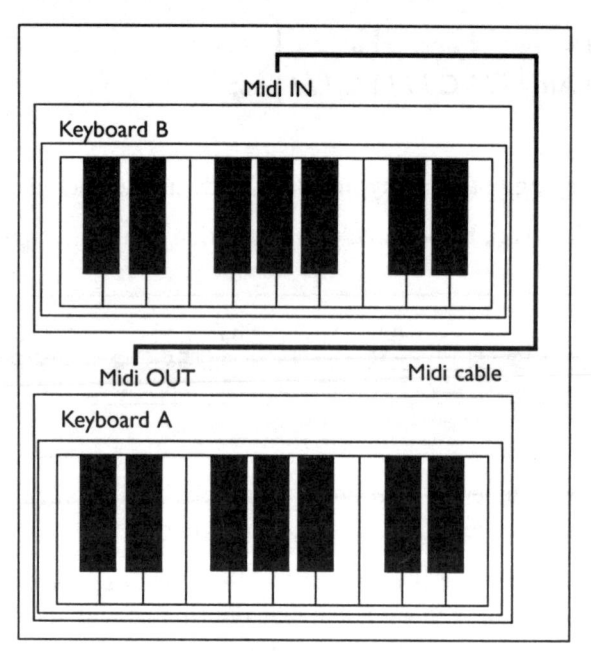

```
                    ┌─────────────────────────┐
                    │      Midi IN            │
            ┌───────┴─────────────────────┐   │
            │ Keyboard B                  │   │
            │  ┌───────────────────────┐  │   │
            │  │ [keyboard keys]       │  │   │
            │  └───────────────────────┘  │   │
            └─────────────────────────────┘   │
                    │                         │
                 Midi OUT        Midi cable   │
            ┌───────┴─────────────────────────┘
            │ Keyboard A                  │
            │  ┌───────────────────────┐  │
            │  │ [keyboard keys]       │  │
            │  └───────────────────────┘  │
            └─────────────────────────────┘
```

Midi Connections

With the Midi connection in place, notes played on keyboard A will concurrently sound on keyboard B. Explore this as a way of combining one sound with another. (Piano and strings, trumpet and saxophone, glockenspiel and guitar etc.) Changing the voice on keyboard A may simultaneously change the sound on keyboard B. Playing notes from one instrument to another uses 'keying information' and the changing of sounds is called 'voice information' – just two of the many types of data it is possible to send, receive or pass on via a Midi connection. The word 'possible' is important because most devices allow only a limited number of Midi possibilities.

Midi Channels

Midi information employs a channel system just as a TV set does. We are accustomed to having a number of channels to choose from. When we click on a channel we can watch the picture, hear the sound and receive the teletext on just that one channel. We know the other channels are being transmitted but we have not selected them. Midi works in a similar way. Information is transmitted and received on up to 16 channels. The transmit and receive channels must correspond to allow the information to flow from keyboard to keyboard. If a Midi connection fails to operate, explore this area first. Methods for changing Midi transmit and receive channels are specific to each instrument.

Other Musical Equipment Utilising Midi

Midi, although starting out as a keyboard device, now has a number of different forms of operation not requiring keyboard skills:

Sound Beams

Ultrasonic beams which will trigger different Midi notes related to space and distance. Great potential for relating any movement to sound. A keyboard or sound module is required.

Drum Pads

A variety of drum pads designed to be hit with hands or sticks. These pads will produce drum sounds but can also be assigned to different notes or sounds of your choice.

Midi Creator

A multi-purpose device which accepts a variety of sensors to convert physical movement into musical sounds. An excellent unit for those working in SLD, PMLD and PD locations. The unit will also accept many existing switches from these areas of work. A keyboard or sound module is required.

Mallet Instruments

Electronic versions of a xylophone, allowing most electronic voices to be played using beaters on flat bar shapes. Amplifier and speakers are required .

Voice Converters

This device uses a microphone and works on the principle of converting a sung note into a Midi note. It is difficult to use. A keyboard or sound module is required.

Guitar Units

A device sensing the notes being played on a guitar and converting them to Midi signals. Amplifier and speakers are required. Some also require a sound module.

Wind Instruments

Instruments requiring fingering and blowing, similar to a recorder. Some can be altered to play different finger positions simulating flute, clarinet, saxophone, etc. Amplifier and speakers are required.

Synthesizers

Keyboard instruments dedicated to producing many high quality sounds which can be changed, edited and remembered. Amplification required.

Sequencers

A device which records Midi information and is able to multi-track music as described earlier but without tape. Recording can be done at a slow speed and then be played back faster. Very useful! Each part is recorded on a different Midi channel with a different voice. Amplifier and sound module required.

Workstations

A keyboard, synthesizer, amplifier and sequencer in the same case.

Sound Modules

Units containing many high quality voices – keyboard sounds without the keys! They are suitable for connecting to computers and/or adding to keyboards via Midi connections. Sound modules are capable of producing more than one voice. Eight or sixteen voices at one time are not uncommon: these are 'multi-timbral'. Amplifier and speakers are required.

Popular computers are capable of making music. Most will require the addition of Midi sockets. With the correct software packages a computer will imitate many of the devices listed.

Hi-tech equipment does provide an approach which attracts many young people into making music but the advances in electronics tend to produce equipment of an abstract nature. This presents difficulties in understanding the internal workings in relationship to the musical context.

CHAPTER 5

Special Learners

The styles and approaches used throughout this book contain many elements firmly based on extensive practice with 'young people' of all ages who have learning difficulties. Music has always provided an excellent and unique tool in this context. The philosophy and method may vary, but the content – music – remains the same.

Understand and share in the depth of feeling attainable through basic music making, the joy it brings and the special affection it holds for many young people. The educational context constantly changes in line with current trends. Working with young people with learning difficulties demands a careful observation of the individual in order to provide a personalised approach irrespective of the context. This is a challenge for all of us.

Learning difficulties have physiological and psychological root causes, are seldom restricted to one area and are likely to affect:

Attention	Attitude	Behaviour
Emotions	Intelligence	Language
Learning	Memory	Motivation
Motor control	Perception	Personality
Physical aspects	Sensory	Socialization

These provide our general areas of focus for work and development. For instance, a group aiming to develop social skills could be working on the sharing and playing together aspect of music, whilst a physical focus could be directed towards the mechanics of producing sounds at a specific point in time. Be conscious of how this reflects a person-centred approach as opposed to a subject-based approach. Many young people will have been deprived of sensory experiences. This may affect their touch, vision, taste, smell, movement and hearing. All of these sensory aspects require consideration and review.

Within any situation it is imperative to assess an individual's strengths, to get to know 'what a person can do'. The strengths are the positives which require celebrating, they become the foundation for development. One positive attitude leads on to the next in a spiral of success. If you look for problems they will gradually overwhelm you! First and foremost, young people are individuals each with a name, personality and character. That they may have a condition which results in learning difficulties or special educational needs comes a distant second.

Labels can sometimes be less than helpful (abilities vary widely within any tag) whilst other broad labels are complex, non-specific jargon. Sometimes the focus of our work will be based on our own assessment of basic abilities such as walking, talking, communication of feelings and wishes, understanding, responding, appropriate behaviour and ability to carry out intentions. Ultimately we may seek out appropriate professional help. Direction, related to the current position and possible future progress, is called for. Do not dismiss yourself from this process. Listen hard to parents, colleagues and other professionals. It is important to realise how vital the people around young persons with learning difficulties are. They need to communicate with each other in an open and frank way, sharing successes and doubts alike. This becomes a powerful collective resource.

There are no quick fixes or easy solutions. Questions are answered by more questions. Consistent high quality teaching is required along with quality experiences and open-ended opportunities. This work places high demands on teachers at physical, emotional and intellectual levels. Endless hours of work searching for a point of contact or a baseline may be required – somewhere to begin.

Music becomes a buoyant activity within this context, capable of offering a refreshing level of optimism. The following example illustrates some of these points. It describes a musical episode in the life of an eight-year-old. This and the other examples are based on true events; names and other fine details have been changed to provide anonymity:

Lisa

Lisa's description would place her as a child experiencing severe learning difficulties of a multiple and profound nature. She has severe grand mal epilepsy, low general muscle tone, flaccid and hypotonic posture, limited mobility, no verbal language or easily recognisable communication system.

Lisa came into a music session where an echo chamber was set up to provide a sound environment. It was possible for her to hear and focus on her own sounds. She made one of her moaning utterances and then heard herself in the reflected echo. Her sound rate increased and each individual utterance became longer with a more defined pitch element.

The note was identified on the piano (F above middle C). We sang her note, played her note, added chords to her note and marvelled at the way she 'fine tuned' her utterance until the note was held in accurate pitch. At the same time Lisa took control of her head and held it up; her face changed to a happy expression. The activity lasted for 45 minutes before fatigue overcame her. This was a very special day for Lisa and also for those who were around her at the time. Her achievements were astounding.

This powerful story contains a number of important points: Lisa used her voice to 'make a mark' in this world of ours. We perceived, from this one piece of work, so much about her levels of understanding, awareness, vocal control, endurance, concentration and her potential to be happy. Little of this had been apparent before the session.

First Instrumental Encounters

'Making your mark' is a very important activity for human beings. Most of us achieve this without sparing a thought. For some of our young people it can be an immensely difficult statement to make. Attempts may be frustrated by any number of factors, leading to introversion and/or anti-social behaviour. For those with communication and motor difficulties, music and musical instruments provide outlets for developing personal identity. Established instrumentalists equally possess a similar extension to their personality. Exploring a wide range of instruments and trying them out is an easy activity, yet a vital way of providing access into a common, communal activity.

To make sounds from instruments is the prime objective of early instrumental work. Maracas, drums, tambourines, tambours, xylophones, chimes as well as suspended spoons, biscuit tins, saucepans and wooden boxes all have an important role for 'mark making'. Additional care should be exercised to encourage all attempts at playing. Exposure to general failure compounds the problems for young people who may be emotionally delicate, vulnerable or lacking in confidence when they enter our doors. All their efforts must be treated with the utmost respect and regard.

Copying, Imitation and Mirroring

Once an individual is playing, development employs turn-taking, copying, imitation and mirroring techniques. The music emanating from an individual is of major significance – this has to be granted the opportunity to flow with acceptance and without judgement. (True for most music making individuals!) Music possesses the ability to strike close to the heart of the human psyche; this accounts for its power over our feelings, thoughts and emotions. These factors demand increased levels of sensitivity, empathy and understanding.

Try these techniques for instigating and developing instrumental work.

Copying

Start by copying whatever comes from the individual. Include body language and style of playing as well as rhythm and pitch. Young people with autism enjoy this activity and usually set complex patterns to be copied. The acknowledgement of a young person's ability to effect the behaviour of an adult has a part to play in this exercise. It is a positive experience for the teacher to be manipulated within this constructive context. Allow initiatives to flow from the young person.

You play – I play

In your playing aim for a similar emotional flavour and respond in a related way to what has been played.

Question and Answer

Build longer phrases for the questions and answers. Accomplished by the use of flow and interesting rhythm.

Rickiel

There are occasions when turn-taking evolves into intricate musical composition, illustrated here by Rickiel, a 10-year-old attending his local primary school. He is a very active, bright character, displaying mildly autistic tendencies, with the ability to use verbal communication though often with limited understanding.

Rickiel and I would improvise together using the pentatonic scale, Rickiel playing on a bass xylophone. It was always wise to remove the relevant bars out of his sight, to avoid him removing all the other bars.

This was not an easy task as little escaped his notice. A particular delight was having two beaters. He was able to handle them well – the instrument possessed bars which were of a sufficient size for him to hit cleanly. Rickiel was an eager musician. His music would naturally begin, I would follow his mood and style on the piano. He usually started in 4/4 time with a fairly brisk tempo. Periodically he would 'throw in' four bars of 3/4. This was his surprise and always resulted in screams of delight from him when I responded by following his change of pulse. His ability to change time from four to three and back to four was always expertly accomplished. The duration of his improvisation would be approximately 20 minutes, his maximum level of concentration. His playing captured flow and spontaneity of thought over a prolonged period, attributes he displayed best within this context.

The musical content of his sessions was based entirely on pentatonic improvisation employing regular rhythm patterns and strong pulses, techniques discussed in previous chapters. Experiences of this nature demonstrate how we need to consider all musical activities to be an entitlement. Music is not an embellishment, treat or extra, nor is it a pleasure to be withdrawn in any form of behavioural modification programme. There is an onus on us to be creative and inventive in order to gain musical access for everyone. Always aim to provide a rich experience.

No Pulse

Some parts of music making should be free from any regular pulse or rhythm particularly if the young people are unable to deliver such things. Design activities with a level of differentiation to cater for a broad range of abilities. Story lines are extremely useful for this type of work, facilitating variety and mixed levels of musical complexity. Here is a simple story for instruments based on a visit to the zoo. Narration is incorporated alongside instruments to add additional stress and meaning to both the spoken and musical language, important aspects of language development:

- *The sun began to rise in the sky.* A cymbal roll gradually becoming louder
- *A bird sang a new song as it sat and watched the sun.* A water-filled whistle (nightingale call) warbling, with recorders adding tune notes. Sticky tape can be placed over the holes on two recorders enabling them to play two single notes which go together pleasantly. More

complex tune ideas should be employed according to ability.
- *The sun shone down on the waters of the lake.* Hands strumming piano strings with sustain pedal jammed down to allow the notes to reverberate.
- *Every day, at this time, the animals came for a refreshing drink. The first to arrive was the . . .* And so the story continues. Everyone chooses their own animal, instrument and level of complexity.

A succession of animals can be played by instruments in turn. Ideas coming from the young people are the best. However, some will not come up with their own ideas immediately – allow them time. Remember, we are not worshipping in the cathedral of correct answers, we are looking for musical representations not sound effects. Understand how one young person can comfortably play a cymbal with great sensitivity and feeling, whilst another plays a complex tune alongside. This level of empathy is common throughout all corporate music making.

An Everyday Context

There will be occasions when the need for more basic subject material presents itself. A less exotic piece using similar techniques could be created depicting the contents of a clothes cupboard.

Object	Instrument
Woolly hat	Small metal instruments
Table cloth	Cup and spoon
Football socks	Whistle, rattle and vocal cheers
Trousers	Maracas

Some will be prompted into playing by seeing the real article, others can relate to pictures, yet others will be able to use memory to imagine the contents of the cupboard. Different options for contrasting young people. Instruments could play as each item dances in the air!

Items could be placed in an imaginative context to tell a story, a fanciful context used as a framework for improvisation:

- The woolly hat musically recounts a walk on a frosty night.
- The table cloth is about a special meal last Thursday.
- The football socks tell of the game last weekend.
- The trousers have sand in the turn-ups from a walk in the old, disused quarry.

Realise the potential for cross arts work within this style of composition – plays, puppets, masks and story books all provide starting points. Notice how reinforcement can be incorporated for clothing items, days of the week, animal names, time and so on. Music used in this way can also become an additional tool for presenting the same information in a new context, ideal for those who need a high repetition rate.

Third Person Instruments

Musical instruments are able to take on the role of an imaginary third person, a quality also of puppets and masks. People can project themselves to others through playing an instrument. The technique acts rather like a layer of protection around the psyche. Using instruments in this way permits some players to project beyond their normal state and is useful for those who are stressed by social situations.

Imagine a group of children who have moderate learning difficulties stemming from disparate conditions. The group includes two who have elected to be mute, four with developmental scars as a result of physical and emotional abuse, three who have epileptic seizures, and so on. There are twelve in all ranging from nine to eleven years of age. Some of these children have been badly abused, let down by the adults in their home life. They seem a demanding group, difficult to motivate and deeply affected by their conditions. Not surprisingly they are finding it hard to make intellectual and emotional progress. It is clear the children are animated by musical instruments, they speak through the instruments and are stimulated by rhythm and rhyme. They can play chord changes and enjoy singing. A glove puppet becomes a constant aid and companion within the classroom, greatly assisting the children to overcome their timid approach to life. They read, play music and talk to the puppet more readily than to the puppeteer. The puppet is always recognised as a safe intermediary.

Children's television uses this powerful mixture of puppets, stories, music and song – programme producers know the success of such combinations. Develop your ideas with substance and direction appropriate to your particular age group, without losing sight of these helpful techniques. Puppets are not exclusive to young children.

Everyday events within the immediate experience of the young people are useful for consolidating work in other curriculum areas. At other times you may wish to create musical stories designed to extend people beyond the immediate realms of their experience. Be it fact, fiction or fantasy, the ideas expressed by young people always provide a suitable level of appropriateness to this work. It stimulates the imagination and feeds the intellect within the most demanding of teaching situations.

Singing

Songs and singing provide a powerful medium and should be developed whenever possible. The world is full of songs covering every imaginable topic. Search them out. Find songs which are suitable for the young people you work with, compose your own and develop an ever-increasing repertoire. Encourage vocal work and develop an ethos which promotes participation without value judgements. Quality can be improved by supporting careful listening and copying opportunities as part of a developmental process.

Here is a list of some positive attributes of singing. You will be able to add more:

- Singing encourages vocal modulation. Meaning is given in language to some extent by changing the pitch of the voice (minor and major thirds are popular).
- Most people, to a greater or lesser extent, tend to read facial expressions and voice intonation, particularly when the words themselves are not understood. Singing usually presents a happy and non-threatening voice to such people – it is difficult to interpret a singing voice as threatening.
- Songs are consistent. Things happen at the same place and time and in the same way. Place and order provide security and a feeling of 'I know this'.
- Songs are repetitious, but things can be repeated without becoming tedious or monotonous.
- Songs are excellent at uniting people for a common cause and understanding. (Congregational singers and football crowds understand this unity.) Assemblies, camp fires, bus journeys, walking – any shared experience is enhanced by songs and singing.
- Singing is a very immediate activity. The basic equipment is close at hand and can be readily adapted to any situation. A handy activity for that spare five minutes!
- Songs demand a reasonable level of thought rate whilst combining listening and participating skills at the same time.
- Some young people will sing words they cannot articulate under any other circumstances.
- Singing is a happy, fun activity.

Singing 'Off the Cuff'

It is great fun to make your own songs up 'as you go along'. Tune, rhyming, rhythm and phrasing are not particularly important in this exercise. Just let it flow. Sing about food, the weather, who is here, or what is happening today. You will need to build your own confidence and gain the support of colleagues. (Assure them you have not gone mad.) This is a useful tool for reaching some young people. Try singing instructions – just let it happen 'off the top of your head'. It creates a positive style of work banter.

A circle activity originated from this kind of improvisation. The young people involved were developing self awareness and group interaction. The song went like this:

[Musical notation for "Pass The Mirror" with lyrics: "Pass the mirror round. Wait for a turn. Look! I can see you. It's David! It's David! We can see you. It's David! It's David! We can see you."]

Pass The Mirror

The actions (passing the unbreakable mirror) and timing are all important. 'Look I can see you' requires precise eye contact with the individual through the mirror, at the exact moment in the song.

Develop a repertoire of songs with a copying structure if you are working with people who have limited reading capacity. Such songs provide an ideal way of including people without having to acknowledge this known area of difficulty. Work songs and spirituals sometimes make use of this technique by incorporating a 'leader and follower' structure. Try writing a copy song of your own. The following example stemmed from a group who where baking birthday cakes. Poetic licence was used in the lyric writing, although there remained a strong association between the direct baking experience and the imaginative context of the song. (A bakery producing a batch of 1000 cakes!) A teenage member of the group was the song leader. Visual props helped him to remember the order of events. (A full version of this song appears in Appendix 2.)

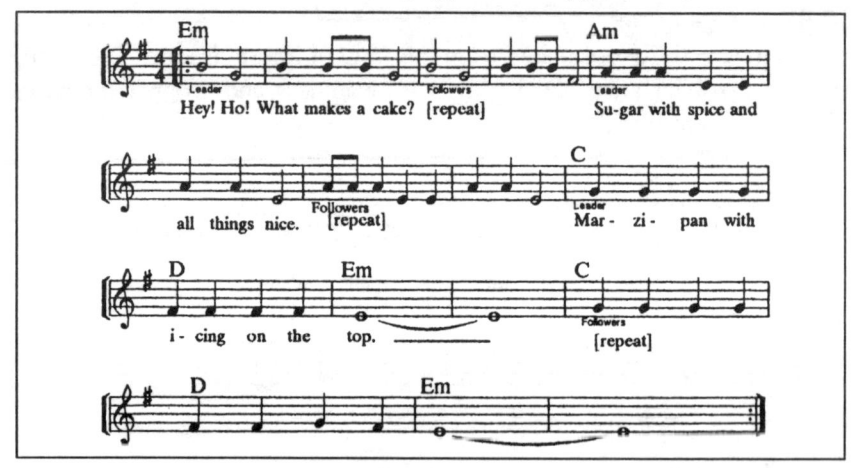

[Musical notation: Em - "Hey! Ho! What makes a cake? [repeat]" (Leader/Followers), Am - "Su-gar with spice and all things nice. [repeat]", C - "Mar-zi-pan with i-cing on the top.", D Em C [repeat], D Em]

A pattern, including minor harmonies with a country-style guitar accompaniment, added to the song's appeal for older students.

The Diminished Individual

There are some young people who battle against a delicate emotional state. Some of them can sense a failure situation long before it happens. This is very common with those who experience learning difficulties. Avoidance strategies are also employed. These possess the potential to become extremely negative in origin and can be destructive to themselves and others. A personal aim can be to avoid getting into situations which trigger failure.

Music can become an exciting new beginning. Types of intelligence, as discussed in Chapter 6, may help to explain the notion of a 'new beginning'. This concept could possibly appeal to different parts of the intellect, never previously explored by the individual. Music will certainly refresh those who perceive they are offered an intense diet in their weaker areas.

Goals should be realistic and reachable. If you can keep the success factor high, individuals are less likely to be stressed. Subsequently they become more successful in an upward spiral. Success is caught and nurtured by this process. The spin-off received by developing young people is tremendous; improvement and development in other curriculum areas tend to follow a general upward trend. The opposite route is a quick cascade towards introversion, anger and frustration.

Stephen

At fourteen years of age, Stephen was very 'street-wise'. He displayed frequent outbursts of verbal and aggressive behaviour – he had a short fuse. Stephen lived in a specialised residential placement and usually related in a negative way to his peer group and the adults around him. He became fascinated by the piano. (Look out for fascination with musical things and use them to the full.) His interest shifted towards an electronic keyboard. Stephen's repertoire included three tunes from memory and he was able to pick out a tune for himself. We started to explore the rhythm/autochord playing aspects of the instrument; this further appealed to him. His attachment to the instrument became greater as the weeks went by. He enjoyed being in the room promptly and always ensured the keyboard was set up and ready.

We improvised around chord sequences and modes (exactly as described in Chapter 4) and he began to make up his own pieces. If anyone entered the room his music would stop until they had gone. So hard was his image, it was clearly difficult for him to be perceived as cooperative and enjoying himself. I would join in with him on another instrument (guitar, another keyboard, electronic wind instrument or piano). We shared the music together and also the little conversations, during and in between the playing. These were the times when he told of his life and how some key adults around him had let him down. Most of his behaviour became understandable as his story unfolded.

Stephen was experiencing a new beginning and was gaining success. Before long reports came telling how well he was doing generally. He was always cooperative, polite and well adjusted for all the music sessions. These delightful lessons took place at a comprehensive school, part of a programme designed to return the young man to 'normality'. It was a pleasure to observe his confidence develop. His efforts were channelled in a positive direction, reducing his need to use anger and aggression as manipulative strategies.

There are many young people who have been badly damaged by events in life. Repairing such scars is a challenging job, every step forward is often the product of painstaking effort for teacher and pupil. Music is particularly rewarding for young people with emotional and behavioural difficulties. Be prepared for them to express deep thoughts and emotions. (This can include the disclosure of abuse.) The success described in Stephen's case can be developed equally in group situations. There are a number of factors worthy of note.

- Detach any negative behavioural patterns from the individual's psyche. A person who feels injured or disliked can resort to behaviour designed to gain attention at almost any price. Closely coupled to this is the need to positively endorse good work and behaviour. Be genuine and protective towards the integrity of the individual.
- Avoid facing negative behaviour with further negative attitudes. Use equipment which will stand up to hard use and take a view which supports instruments to be an entitlement, similar to food and clothing. Explore home-made instruments. When young people have been denied many things, taking more away from them has little positive value. Others will have experienced verbal aggression well beyond any level we may display in our worst moments. Threats and fear are extremely poor servants and cannot be allowed to hold any place in positive learning strategies.
- Always aim to be consistent and fair. Young people with emotional and behavioural problems have a rather over-zealous attitude towards situations they regard as unfair They will always desire an instrument given to someone else. Make sure equipment changes hands frequently within sessions. The picture cards of instruments mentioned in Chapter 3 (p.32) provide a useful 'chance' way of handling instruments. Other chance techniques should be employed because they are perceived to be fair and even handed. Sand timers can be used. The music lasts until the sand has finished. A large stop-watch may be used in the same way.
- Pace a session by using a number of varied activities. Try keeping the smaller instruments in a box or suitcase. At the end of a piece of instrumental work the instruments can be returned to the case and then a song or listening game can begin. A return to the instrumental work starts with opening up the case symbolising a new beginning. A half-hour music session may require three or four 'new beginnings'.
- Develop a model for both work and behaviour which provides limited help on demand.
- Remember to ask about the content of musical compositions before they are performed. Guessing games are not particularly helpful and can become hopelessly inaccurate compared to the ideas within the players' minds.

A Point and Play Machine

This machine has proved to be useful in establishing fair turn-taking. Find an old musical box and remove the metal comb which provides the notes (usually held by two screws). Cut out a pointer from a large plastic ice cream container and find a way of firmly securing it to the winder of the musical box. (Very strong glue.) Set the musical box going. The remaining mechanism will govern the clockwork, permitting it to slowly unwind; the pointer will rotate as this happens. The game is: play your instrument for as long as the pointer is directed at you. Work in a circle around the device. As the clockwork runs down the playing turns become longer.

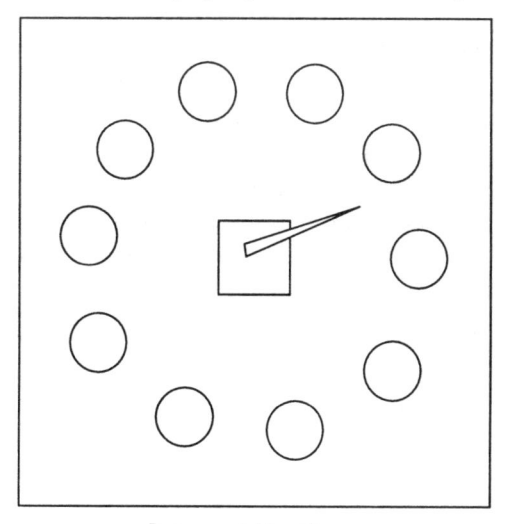

Point and Play Game

A Learning Model: Limited Help on Demand

Remember how Goldilocks liked everything: not too hot, not too cold, but just right. All things were required to be 'just right'. 'Limited help on demand' relates to interactions with young people. Our efforts need to be 'just right'. If we help and control all the time, then our intervention is too great and the individual's learning is always subject to the terms and conditions set down by our controlling influence. This situation is demonstrated by the teacher who acts as the strict disciplinarian using the approach of, 'First you must do this, then that, followed by . . .' Individuals consider themselves to be helpless and learn more about helplessness within this context. Real learning is limited in nature. Equally, the teacher who intervenes on the young person's behalf and assists at every conceivable moment also endorses these thoughts. The examples tend to indicate situations where the adult is fulfilling their own needs. The opposite end of this continuum is total freedom: 'Do what you like it doesn't matter' or 'go away and come back with a piece of music about . . . !' This approach develops a sort of chaos within the individual, feelings of 'Anything goes,' or 'It doesn't matter' are fostered.

Our ultimate goal should be to achieve limited help on demand. This requires individuals to work at the task, discover for themselves, yet be given just sufficient help to send them in the most appropriate direction for achieving an acceptable result. This requires an amount of personal responsibility from the student. Extra demands are placed on us to avoid over-involvement in the learning process. This approach, unfortunately, can rapidly be perceived as insufficiently 'schoolly' for some colleagues. It does establish solid principles for life and holds true as an attitude to adopt for both academic and behavioural purposes. It ultimately encourages individuals to take responsibility for themselves.

If the young people lack ideas, or express a reluctance to present them, interjections from adults may initially be greater. Gradually reduce the adult input until they gain confidence in their own ideas. Remember to let go as soon as possible!

Some useful open-ended questions to ask are:

- Have you thought about . . . ?'
- What do you think happens next . . . ?'
- What could you do with . . . ?'

The challenges we face from young people with learning difficulties will always demand a considerable amount of personal reflection. Maintain the integrity of the students, keep them intact and build them up as individuals. Consider these psychological aspects to be more significant than specific musical development.

Music therapy has long acknowledged the use of music as a tool to achieve non-musical aims. Music will penetrate deeply in a way which will stir hearts and minds. Time directed towards creating a suitable dynamic will be productive. To enable this process, young people need to detect trust within the framework of each relationship. Interpersonal relationships are a crucial key to success. Additional strategies can be employed to bring this about.

- Aim to teach the making of good choices – choice of instruments, choice of composition content, choice of dynamic content. Naturally at the hub of choice is the presentation of options from which to choose. Allow time for this to happen.

- Adopt strategies to spread the 'leader' role amongst the group.
- Accept good ideas whilst at the same time realising that the ideas do not have to exactly correspond to your own. (What colour are trees? Green is only one of many acceptable answers.)
- Young people may not understand the words or language being used; few people actually understand from a one-off chance. Expect to say things more than once and in different ways. A cliché teacher line is 'How many times do you need telling . . . !' Of course the wise answer is 'As many times as it takes for me to understand!'
- Music has a delightful social aspect, quickly binding people together with shared aims. Use music in this way.
- Design work which develops a problem-solving flavour. How can you make the piece longer? What would happen if the drum was played with finger tips instead of sticks? Can you play your tune pattern higher?
- A basic and important aspect of every music session is to acknowledge each individual and to call them by name.
- Expect to be changed within a session. The journey of learning is a shared experience between students and teacher which requires mutual empathy and understanding.
- Enjoy and celebrate the learning experience of the present moment. Some young people have conditions which do not provide them with endless time. Extra quality is required for all events.

A Greeting Song (see p.84)

A strong rock feel added to simple words serves as an effective way to acknowledge everyone. This presents a positive start to music sessions. Melodic and vocal repetition make it an easy song for the singer. Greeting is an important ritual of human behaviour. Songs such as this provide an effective way to acknowledge the group and its members.

Further Factors

- Be as consistent as possible.
- Analyse and review what you are doing and why you are doing it on a regular basis.
- Be organised (even more than usual).
- Carefully analyse activities and be prepared to break them down into smaller manageable units.
- Quick-fix solutions do not exist. Be prepared to examine fundamental attitudes and techniques.

A Greeting Song

Specialised Equipment

Large instruments producing low frequencies are very desirable for all levels of work. They present large surface areas for making contact and produce additional tactile sound qualities. Most other equipment is exactly the same as in any situation for creating music; adaptations tend to be geared to specific individual needs. These are a few of my own favourites which have been indispensable over the years. Young people have always derived an immense amount of pleasure from them.

- A large 24-inch diameter bass drum with one skin. Great for playing,

great for feeling vibrations, large enough to hit easily and loud enough to create a big sound when required.
- A large 20-inch diameter cymbal. Big, brash and bright. A very exciting instrument visually and aurally.
- A bass xylophone. Big bars, beautiful round sound, good for ostinati and drones.
- A set of chimes (commercial version of the home made ones described in Chapter 8). They are very easy to play and their simple sound carries the imagination for a million miles!
- A guitar and a piano accordion. Portable instruments enabling physical movement and direct contact with the group. The combination of the two instruments provides a contrast in tones and facilitates different styles of accompaniment.

Music is My First Love

Once upon a time there was a young person who experienced severe language and communication problems, his home circumstances were far from ideal and he attended a residential special school. Despite a vast amount of specialist language work, his level of verbal communication remained limited. His preferred communication was to play a small 'penny whistle'. He played simple tunes which haunted the air, making his mark in our world. He was spontaneous and totally engaged in this activity. Music was his first love, it was his most fluent and expressive form of communication. The sad part of this story lies in the way he waited for others to realise how his humble music playing was more crucial to him than anything else. He was searching for musicians who would change the rules of our music conventions. For him there could be no music examinations, no ensemble group, no orchestra, no public performance, no selection process he could pass. His interest, enthusiasm and need for music were paramount. He is one of many young people who have similar aptitudes and experiences.

Please do not leave those with learning difficulties out in the cold. Find ways of changing the conventional rules and change yourself in ways which will help such young people to be fully included, able to reach their full potential. This is their great unspoken expectation of us. In return they will become our great teachers, capable of introducing us to their subtle yet profound lessons. There is a tacit challenge for all of us to think, and then think again, of ways to build an art form within a society which fosters true acceptance as a basic premise. The road is long.

CHAPTER 6

Developing Creativity and Imagination

Creativity is a basic human activity which requires fostering and nurture. Unfortunately, our society is slow to recognise the importance of creativity as a fundamental skill. The first sound played, the first word written on a page, the first utterance of a conversation – all require our creative thought processes to be engaged. But an initial burst of energy is required to initiate momentum. Creative thoughts are also capable of challenging our previous perception in all situations. Without them our world would be deprived of innovation and invention. It is a form of intelligence which responds to training and development.

Within music we are familiar with the re-creative process – playing a piece or singing a song composed by another person. Musicians become extremely skilful at interpreting the ideas of others. Creation and re-creation are related yet different. Re-creation should be adopted not as a pedagogic structure but as part of the skill-building and knowledge base which support our own originality.

Creativity appears to have a direct relationship with imagination, a notion of transforming dreams into reality. This in turn links with known levels of understanding to make the reality viable. All culminates in an expression of thoughts and ideas.

Young people are full of imagination, which is affiliated to the developing sense of perception. Early perception provides a prismatic view of life in which mental images are different to reality. View the works of art adorning school walls and notice how sharp images, in vivid colour, reveal a world of such transposed images. They demonstrate an incongruous relationship between size, perspective and fine detail. Many of these works of art are produced with a minimum of adult intervention. The artist is progressing through known stages of the art form. Encouragement and confidence building are part of the teacher's primary function in this work.

These fundamental techniques are not to be underestimated. The early artist employs these methods to explore the world of developing perceptions of colour, texture, shape, materials and technique. These are constituent parts of a visual art form.

Music has equivalent qualities and components requiring a hands-on approach. As musicians, we are required to gain insight, understanding, acceptance and the potential for changed levels of perception, within a musical context. Currently we operate a system which mistakenly measures young people alongside those who display prodigious levels of musical perception – the equivalent of comparing a Lowry with a stick drawing produced by a seven-year-old. Most of our work will involve the production of the musical equivalents of early art. They form examples clearly identifiable as part of early development, whilst still having a relationship with the fully mature art form. To be part of self-created music has a rich dimension – it permits exploration of our creative characteristics. Compositions embrace different qualities for the participants, compared to the more objective views of listeners on the outside. Not all creative music immediately conforms to a performer-audience convention; this does not make it of less value.

It is unfair to consider creativity to be an ever-flowing attribute; we have to nurture the process. There will be occasions when we differentiate between creativity and originality; they are not necessarily identical. Observe soap suds in the washing-up bowl, the bubbles merging with neighbouring bubbles. Creative minds tend to handle information in a similar way. They take two pieces of data and amalgamate them into a new format. The individual has total ownership of this new construction.

Within the context of creative music making we are experiencing qualities capable of accessing the inner realms of the human psyche, close to the centre of our very being. Fundamental activities require careful handling; creativity will be destroyed by excessive criticism. Ideas may need to germinate before an individual is sufficiently confident to share them.

The creative process also requires individuals to share their fantasies; this encourages a process by which we mentally rehearse different ideas. These are based on the simulation of experiences and memories from previous sensory stimulation. All minds are involved in this operation, particularly in childhood. We clearly understand the importance of encouraging imaginative play for these very reasons.

Musical creativity involves presenting young people with an opportunity to gain experience in one of the less common modes of learning. Different schools of philosophy and psychology offer a variety of models of intelligence. Howard Gardner specifically refers to music in his list of seven different forms of intelligence – linguistic, logical/mathematical, musical, spatial, bodily/kinaesthetic, interpersonal and intrapersonal. Within this context, formalised education focuses extensively on the first two, but creativity permeates all aspects of intelligence. It is possible for conflict to occur between creative interests and those systems of education based on dogmas of linguistics and logic.

The style proposed and adopted within these pages requires improvisation linked to the teaching of technique and skill-building. This redresses the balance weighted at present in favour of linguistic and logical learning and encompasses broader realms of intellectual development. It aims to provide maximum creative opportunities within a framework of accountability. Creating music becomes an extension of play and continues into the years beyond childhood. There is an interesting association between playing music and childhood play. We use the same word and perhaps it has a similar definition, a notion of sustained effort which feels different to 'work'. This 'play' is rejuvenating, enjoyable, personally motivating and fun. Most play activities masquerade as other occupations in adulthood. Musical instruments are wonderful toys for all ages!

We should hold a personal sadness for those young people who are conditioned to believe music is not 'proper work' and a greater remorse for the attitudes which perpetuate this myth. These are further examples of the delicate balance between the linguistic, logical and musical forms of intelligence. Painting-by-numbers and colouring-in provide shallow examples of this tension. People develop in a holistic fashion only by nurturing all aspects of intelligence. The current imbalance of the equation requires additional input from all creative art forms to redress the balance between left and right brain activity.

Creativity should be fostered and encouraged at every opportunity because of the special qualities it possesses. Ultimately it becomes a personal flair, drawing out individuality and unique qualities within people. Without nurture it withers, but fortunately it can be rekindled. Observe people in their fifties, sixties and seventies working at creative music. Initially they may be reticent owing to some reduction in their willingness, adaptability and malleability. By skilful confidence-building, acceptance and involvement their creativity is rekindled. The content of their work is likely to be early in nature. Within the context of this book they are considered to be 'young people' developing early creative strategies. They dynamically illustrate the difference between music developmental age and chronological age. Their creative development was achieved through opportunity and empowerment. As a reader of this book you are likely to be a key person in providing opportunities for this development, or someone searching for your own opportunities.

Developing creativity does not require the neglect of existing ideas, in fact totally the opposite. Learn from the success of others, examine closely the things they do and how they do them. Observation helps us to understand how to create the important aspects of climate and atmosphere. Become a discerning observer, able to analyse. Once engaged in this process, it becomes possible to observe the difference between teaching strategies designed to benefit the teacher more than pupil, an unfortunate approach we all employ to some degree.

Media Models

The media have become savage consumers of creative music and present many models for ourselves and young people. Much of what we hear is cliché and pastiche. However, by taking note of what is happening we can provide information and ideas and acquire some appropriate role models. All music possesses creative ideas: observe the way music is used to heighten visual effects or manipulate emotions. Copy elements of such ideas and also observe how susceptible we are to fashion. Look out for ideas which could be developed in our work, whilst recognising that some techniques and skills are beyond our scope. Music has the ability to trigger physiological responses, for example changes in pulse, blood pressure and breathing rate. There is a deliberate intention for music to create emotionally charged atmospheres designed to manipulate these autonomic responses.

Points of Creative Focus

The pianist accompanying old silent movies acquired a complete repertoire from concentrating on scenarios. Here are some examples to be developed within the context of our music sessions.

Styles of movement

Creeping, stalking, ambling, walking, running, chasing, pursuing, leaping, gliding, floating, falling, flowing. Could be related to tempo/pulse/beat!

Signature tunes

Tunes associated with specific characters (simplified *Peter and the Wolf* ideas). Jingles, call signs and advertisements make extensive use of this technique. (The BBC use the notes **b**, **b** and **c** as a basis for its musical logo.) Listen out for 'goody' and 'baddy', 'winner' and 'loser' tunes, friendly, hostile or joke music. Discord and concord would achieve this!

Emotional mood music

Happy, sad, peace, calm, fear, anger, rage, danger.

Ethereal music

All used to signal being out of a normal world – in a dream, outer space, stars, under the sea, experiencing a flash-back. Long, sustained sounds. Sometimes whole-tone scale tunes; synthesised sounds of a choral flavour.

Climatic music

Night, dark, daylight, sunshine, wind, storms, rain, snow, hot, cold, dawn.

Time passing music

Seconds, minutes, hours, days, years, centuries, Winter, Summer.

Dramatic action music

Knocking on a door, hitting out, falling over, machines in motion, fights, emergencies.

Location music

Town, city, country, forest, seaside, caves, different countries, cafe, railway station, hospital, market.

Consider these ideas as flavours or essences. Sometimes the intention is to provide the slightest hint of a particular characteristic. Timbre, rhythm, melody, texture, harmony and all the other musical ingredients become the vital tools in achieving these appropriate flavours.

Setting Stories to Music

As you read stories to your groups, begin by adding one or two instruments to role play different characters. The instruments can play anything from a single sound (rattle, shake, bang) through to a complex tune, as the characters appear in the story. Plan in advance the musical ideas, then incorporate them into the story on a given signal. This will allow an amount of licence for a story where the characters appear at every other word.

Orchestral and operatic composers make extensive use of tunes to signal the arrival of characters, things or abstract ideas. (This technique is known as *leitmotif*.)

Carefully consider all the ingredients of music. A xylophone played with soft padded sticks may be a friendly character, whilst hard wooden sticks could depict a harsher personality. There will be times when our young people require the teaching of different skills and techniques, by demonstration and example. Good practice dictates a requirement for the teacher to create music alongside young people, in order to become part of a realistic work model.

Expand the work by musically setting a scene for the story, some music which happens before the story begins – an overture. Construct the overture in a fashion which anticipates the story to come. For example, a story about soldiers could open with a side drum piece through to a full-blown march. Composers initially wrote overtures based around material used later in the opera – many musical snippets woven together. Another idea to employ.

Movement or a change of location is a possible source of inspiration for the next piece of creative music and so we continue by deciding which aspects of the story to focus on. Eventually our overall piece may look like The Overall Plan (see p.92).

No prizes for guessing the story! This simple example illustrates the construction of a musical story. It resembles an adapted rondo. The story becomes the common thread to which we return after each musical excursion. Each section could be a couple of minutes long. The story-telling can occur above one quiet, sustained note or an unusual chord. Handel used solo singers in his oratorios to cover relatively large sections of story, using the minimum of musical ideas in recitative, e.g. *Messiah*).

The content of each creative piece will depend very much on the musical ability of the young people. Perhaps it would be like this:

Composition Ideas

Setting the Scene Music (Dark Forest)

Sombre instruments with 'dark' tonal qualities.
Tuned instruments playing notes from the whole-tone scale.
Un-tuned percussion instruments hinting at insects and animals lurking in the undergrowth: maracas, kokiriko, vibraslap.
Sustained and slow-moving, perhaps without a regular pulse.

The Overall Plan

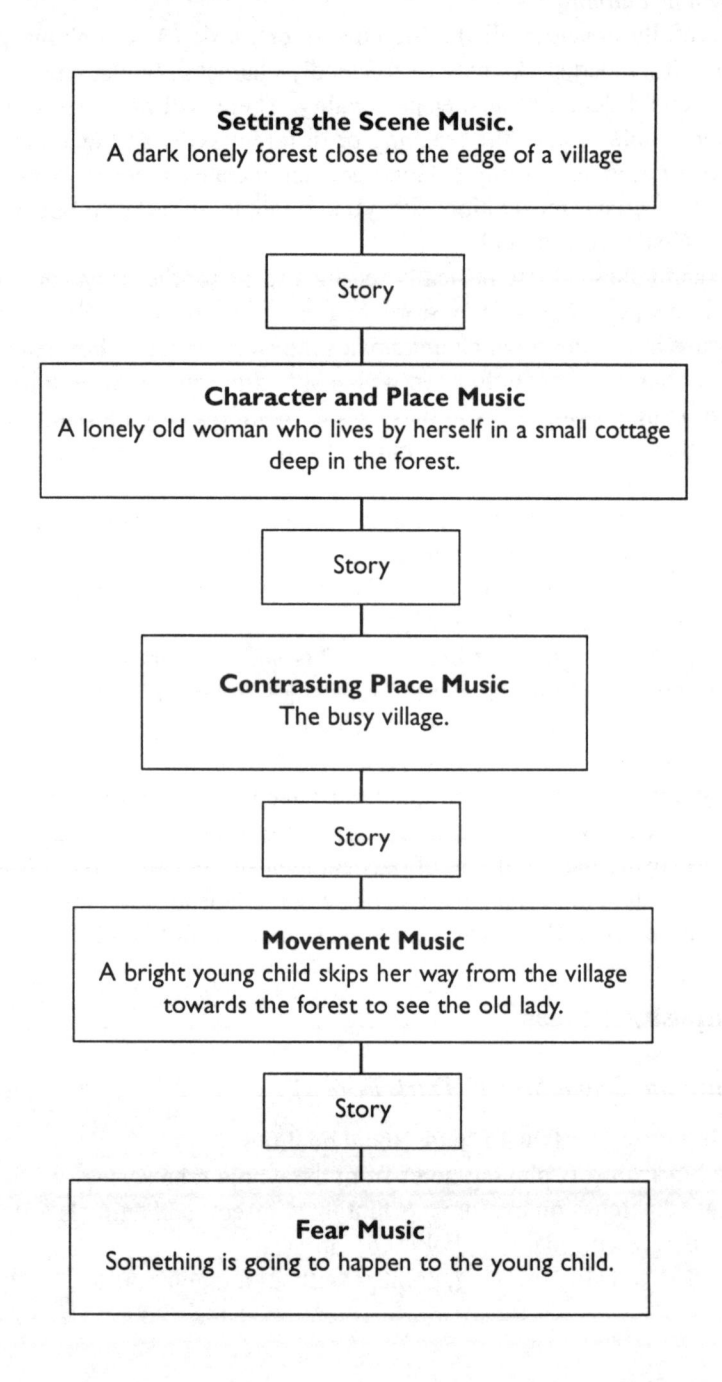

Setting the Scene Music.
A dark lonely forest close to the edge of a village

Story

Character and Place Music
A lonely old woman who lives by herself in a small cottage deep in the forest.

Story

Contrasting Place Music
The busy village.

Story

Movement Music
A bright young child skips her way from the village towards the forest to see the old lady.

Story

Fear Music
Something is going to happen to the young child.

Character Music (Old Woman)

Brittle sounding instruments.
Low sounding, tuned instruments moving at a sedate pace playing an 'old woman' tune.
Un-tuned instruments of a deep tone playing suitable rhythmic accompaniment.

Contrasting Place Music (The Village)

Hustle and bustle depicted by a lively pulse, quick chord changes using a variety of instrumentation.
Repeating rhythm patterns indicative of machines and work. Everything of a busy nature to contrast with the isolation of the forest.

Movement Music (Skipping child.)

This is specifically the young child. A skipping rhythm is required (a fast version of ♩. ♪).
Tuned instruments using a mixture of percussion and recorder or flute, high pitch to contrast with the old woman. (Employing a pentatonic scale?)
Assorted un-tuned percussion picking up on the dotted rhythm.

Fear Music (Something will happen.)

Quiet stroking on the piano strings and sustained cymbal playing, contrasted with sudden, loud sounds from un-tuned percussion. A low drum adding a heart beat.
A discord broken into separate notes played over and over at a high pitch. (a, b♭, c♯, d, c♯, b♭)

Narration Accompaniment

Any low single note. (Bottom **a**.)
Unusual chord/s. (**Am** and **Em** at the same time or **Am** and **D** simultaneously.) The single note and the two unusual chords can be linked together. Experiment with two simple chords played at the same time as a short cut way of achieving compound chords.

A Suite

As an alternative structure use a thematic approach, a suite. Composers have always used suites as a device to assemble collections of matching pieces. A theme loosely based on sailing ships and the sea might broadly look like this:

Sailing
Becalmed
Fish in the sea
A mighty storm
The crew at work

Becalmed

Gentle, sustained sounds from instruments with smooth qualities. A lilting $\frac{3}{4}$ rhythm depicting the motion of a boat. Creaking of rigging sounds – scraped strings. Simple repeating chord pattern (**Am, G**).

Fish in the sea

Play, relating the bright colours of fish to contrast with the darkness of the depths (timbre).
Slow movements of large creatures contrasting with fast sounds of small fish (tempo).

A mighty storm

A gradual introduction of gentle rain and building in vigour and volume with gales and tempest.
Eventually calming down and reversing back to gentle rain (dynamic intensity).

The crew at work

Repetitive rhythmic patterns which are in some way related to physical toil – hauling, lifting, swaying (rhythm).

All music created in this way usually contains basic expressive elements, which in turn require artistic honesty and integrity. Elementary work should include many opportunities to compose sound pictures, illustrate stories or compose music for poems, pictures and paintings. The events described do not have to be particularly profound. A simple journey or other experience shared by the group members becomes valid subject material for a composition. Turgid material can gain a new lease of life through such treatment (early reading books, things we do over and over, things we take for granted).

Writing Songs

There will be times when it is impossible to locate a suitable song for a particular context. Writing your own is a viable option. Throughout this book there are a number of examples of occasions when additional words or songs could be created or developed. Here we focus on the basic principles required. The words in italics make reference to the construction of a specific example.

- A theme is required. What is the song about? (*Flying away on holiday.*)
- Have an idea blitz on words and phrases which are related to the chosen subject. (*Take off, holidays, cloud, climbing, airport, speed, soaring.*)
- Plan an outline for the song. (*Verse – chorus – verse – chorus.*)
- Decide on a metre and construct a rhyming plan for the song, including a pattern for the rhyming required. (*You can copy one from an existing song.*) This folk song has a simple basic structure:

> A nice young man was William *Brown*
> He worked for a wage in a northern *town*.
> He worked from six 'til eight at *night*,
> Turning a wheel from left to *right*.
>
> Chorus Keep that wheel a *turning*,
>   Keep that wheel a *turning*,
>   Keep that wheel a *turning*,
>   And do a little more each day.

Folk Song – William Brown

Rhyming happens in two pairs for the verse. Three lines rhyming and a throw-away line completes the chorus.

- From the word blitz, extract or expand suitable words to rhyme. (*Fly – high – sky – etc.*) Rhyming dictionaries are available!
- Use a known chord pattern or invent your own. (See Chapter 4.)
- Write out the chord pattern and then explore the use of words and phrases. Trial and error is the best way to approach this task.

The Chord Sequence

This is the same chord sequence used in *William Brown*. Rhymes are shown in place:

Verse

| D / / / | A / / / |
           cloud,
| A / / / | D / / / |
           crowd,
| D / / / | A / / / |
           soar,
| A / / / | D / / / |
           roar.

Chorus

| D / / / | A / / / |
           fly,
| A / / / | D / / / |
           sky,
| D / / / | G / / / |
           by,
| A / / / | D / / / |

Working back from the rhymes presents the following lyrics:

Verse

Flying up above the cloud,
We're heading for the fun packed crowd.
Ever up and on we soar.
Surging on, our engines roar.

Chorus

Higher and higher, higher we fly,
Wings out-spread to touch the sky,
Friends below are soon passed by.
We journey on our way.

- Choose a style and speed. Keyboards are a possible source of inspiration. (Party Pop ♩ = 130)
- Begin work on the tune and try out a number of ideas. (Chapter 3)
- The chords, melody, words or any other aspect of the song can be re-worked.

Be careful, the end result could be a number one hit with holiday makers, maybe like this:

Holiday Song

This version illustrates re-working of chords to include minor harmonies:

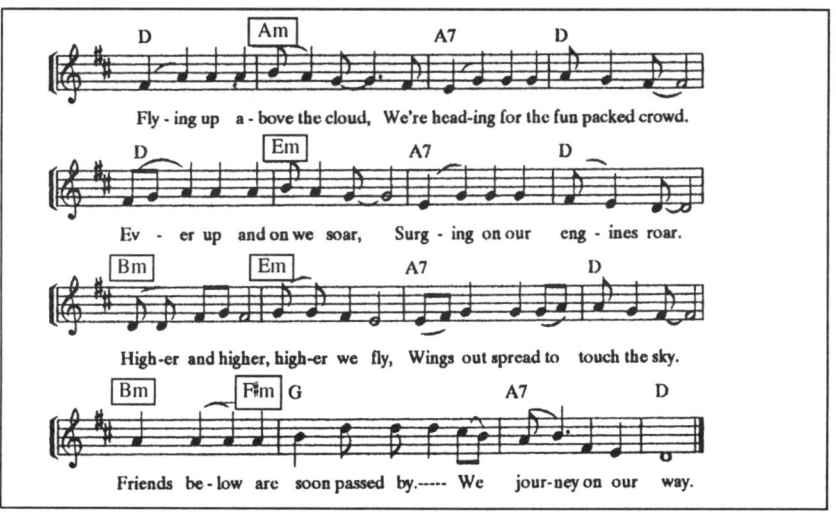

In other chapters we discover explanations of musical grammar, conventions and techniques which provide the knowledge that combines with imagination to develop creativity. The whole exercise becomes a messy business which on occasions defies all types of schematic progress. Learning is often like that! At all times, the creation of music will be positively influenced by good teaching and careful preparation, providing a firm grounding in both knowledge and experience.

CHAPTER 7

Personal Musical Development

People who are interested in music making often express dissatisfaction with their playing ability and other musical skills. However accomplished, we never feel satisfied or we perceive someone else to be more skilful. The word 'talent' also figures in our thoughts, usually with an implied meaning of 'gifts from God'. This interpretation has a negative effect on those who feel they did not receive the gift! Any talent (i.e. great ability) has usually received nurture, extensive teaching, hours of practice and a fairly single-minded level of dedication. Musicians are no exception.

All aspects of music making will be enhanced by motivated learning. Most people do not have prodigious abilities, but strive to do well and to fully develop their skills. This chapter is a collection of ideas and techniques designed for and dedicated to those who wish to discover or re-discover specific musical skills to use in their work. Place all competitive notions behind you and move forward, resolute to progress your own skills. Be prepared to commit time, effort and dedication: these are essential keys to success. Some of the ideas offer short cuts or approach tasks from a different angle in order to achieve rapid access to the skills.

For Everyone

- Review how to attain your musical goals avoiding previous failures.
- Attempt to analyse factors which inhibited your success in the past.
- Be specific and set realistic goals.
- Take control of your own musicality – it is yours.
- Be positive and ask those around you to be positive towards your musical development.

Recapturing Instrumental Skills

- Take your instrument and learn to love it for its own sake. This involves playing, experimenting and generally becoming conversant with it.
- Use some ideas found in other areas of this book to create tunes, rhythms and moods on your instrument.
- Try to establish an ability to play freely on your instrument, to feel relaxed, as you do in conversation with a good friend.
- You may need to find a good teacher, one who will look on you as an individual and who will help you to discover your path of musical development, not theirs.

For Absolute Beginners

Set out to learn an accompaniment type of instrument to use during singing. If you are confident in singing, one of the following instruments could be the choice for you. They all have features designed to reduce the amount of time learning takes. (Usually measured in hours, days or weeks as opposed to years.)

Chromaharp

This instrument has a number of chord bars and works on the basic principle of press the bar at the required point in the tune and strum the strings. (This is a recognised principle used by all accompaniment type instruments.) Words with the chord names over the top become a suitable and quickly understood form of notation for this style of playing.

```
Strum the D7 chord to establish the first note
then:
        | G        | D7
Happy | birthday to | you.
                    | G
Happy | birthday to | you.
                        | C
Happy | birthday dear |_____
        | G      D7 | G
Happy | birthday to | you.
```

Happy Birthday

If you are buying an instrument please remember the following points:

- Most instruments are capable of playing 12 to 15 different chords:

| E♭ | D | F7 | Gm | B♭ | A7 | C7 | Dm | F | E7 | G7 | Am | C | D7 | G |

- An Autoharp is technically a similar instrument. There are many strings on all chordal zithers which are not easy to tune without experience: a 'stable' instrument is preferable. Electronic tuners will help with this.
- An Omnichord is an electronic version of a chordal zither; it is played in the same way. It includes an automatic rhythm section similar to an electronic keyboard.
- In instrument-buying terms the most expensive of chordal zithers will not be excessively expensive.
- People learn to play basic accompaniments very quickly and it is a viable instrument for young people to handle.
- It is portable and has a pleasing acoustic sound.

Piano Accordion

The piano accordion has buttons (played with the left hand) for chords and bass notes. A small keyboard is used for right-handed tune playing. A certain amount of co-ordination is required to operate bellows and hands at the same time! Song accompaniments can be achieved using only the left hand buttons and keyboard skills are not initially required. The buttons are laid out in a fixed pattern, the same for all piano accordions (see diagram on p.101).

Piano accordions are discussed in terms of the number of left hand (bass) buttons. The diagram shows part of the button arrangement. Different vertical rows are used for bass notes, major chords and minor chords. A 48 bass (12 x 4) is a handy size for general use. Do not be alarmed by the number of buttons; many songs can be accompanied by using six in close proximity. You can forget about all the others, perhaps forever! The c bass note is marked with an indentation or a spot as a distinguishing feature. By using the ring finger on this bass note the chord button will be in easy reach of the tallest finger. The horizontal rows are angled to accommodate this. The index finger will eventually play an alternate bass note.

By looking back at the section on chord playing (p.41), you will realise the logical arrangement of buttons for chords I, IV and V. If you keep the relationship of buttons in mind, any chord button you choose can be chord I with chord V always situated as the adjacent chord above and chord IV located immediately below chord I. The arrangement stays the same from

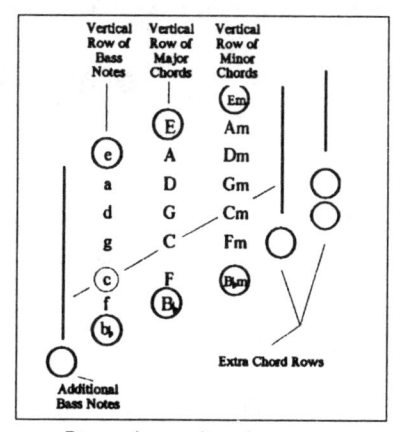

Piano Accordion Layout

the top to the bottom of all the buttons. Major chords are the most common; therefore the row of minor chords can be dismissed for a while. Playing is far less daunting by the dismissal of all but six left-hand buttons:

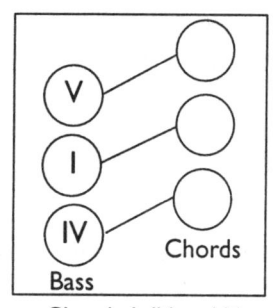

Chords I, IV and V

Young people are captivated by the tonal quality of piano accordion music. It produces a jolly rhythmic feel which sets feet tapping. If this is a skill you choose to develop please consider the following:

- There are old second-hand instruments to be found (make sure all notes/bass buttons play – and stop playing).
- A 48 bass is an adequate number of bass buttons.
- Large instruments may be too heavy for moving around whilst playing.
- It will take a period of dedicated time to develop the co-ordination skills required.
- Some instruments allow you to select different sounds on the keyboard. The sound is produced by metal reeds (the same as a mouth organ). The 'French' sound is achieved by having two reeds for each note with one slightly out of tune with the other. (I shall say this only once.) Spots are used as indicators to signal the selection of reeds, the quantity and octave:

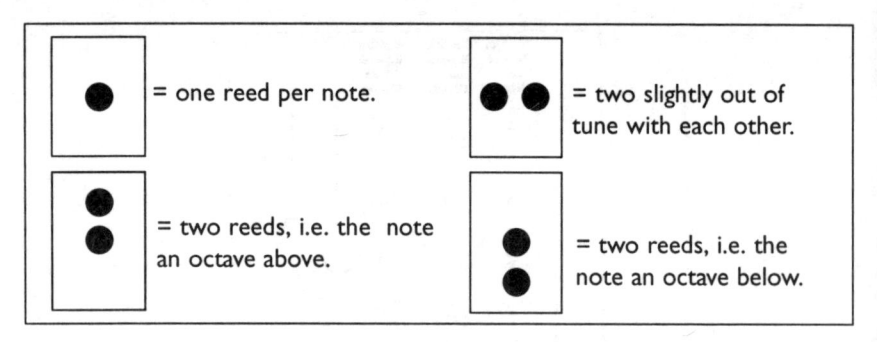

●	= one reed per note.	● ●	= two slightly out of tune with each other.
● ●	= two reeds, i.e. the note an octave above.	● ●	= two reeds, i.e. the note an octave below.

Stops to change the Tone

This explains the code sufficiently for working out other permutations you may find.

When you are ready to incorporate the right hand, begin by playing introductions (see p.107/8) and move on to playing additional notes of the chord on the keyboard.

Piano accordions play the same notes irrespective of the direction of bellow movement. Some melodeons change notes depending on the bellow movement. Similar to a mouth organ, notes change in relationship to sucking or blowing.

Keyboards

Introductory keyboard work is discussed in Chapter 4. Playing keyboards using an autochord system is very similar to piano accordion playing – the left hand operates a type of automatic playing mechanism. Keyboards are designed to permit several levels of interaction. 'Single finger' playing styles are discussed on p.63. A recent development is 'fingered mode' allowing the player to select specific notes in the left hand. The keyboard then processes this information to calculate a bass part and a rhythmic style. If you wish to develop a 'fingered' left hand style it is necessary to build up a vocabulary of left hand chord shapes.

Examine the chord of **C** – it is possible to shuffle the notes into three different options: **c e g, e g c, g c e**. The automatic electronic circuits will read each of these options as a chord of C major. (Larger keyboards analyse left hand notes and display the name of the chord.) Because we can shuffle the order of notes to suit ourselves, aim to change from one chord to the next by moving the minimum number of notes. Look out for notes which are common – they make useful anchors:

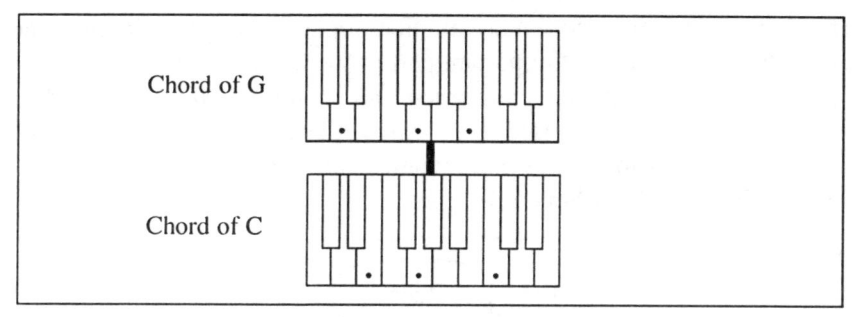

[Diagram: Chord of G (upper keyboard) and Chord of C (lower keyboard)]

Minimum Movement

In this illustration the index finger (**g**) provides an anchor for the left hand. This hand is then able to pivot around that finger as it moves from the chord of **G** to the chord of **C**. Having one constant finger can assist in establishing a more speedy perception of the keyboard. Additional information relating to chords is given in Appendix 3. Visit your local music shop and buy a keyboard book with pictures of all the chords possible. The best way to learn the different chords is by looking up the new ones required for a particular song and gradually building a chord vocabulary, several at a time.

Some points to remember:

- The world is full of under-used keyboards; an extensive second-hand market exists. People fall in love with the idea of playing a keyboard but often experience problems in understanding how to operate it and how it works. An owner's manual is vital.
- The auto play systems can allow access to music making which would not be possible without the technology. They assist in stretching our skills.
- Results can be achieved by investing a relatively short amount of time. Sometimes people who see themselves as failed pianists become re-motivated and successful keyboard players.
- New models appear annually and are packaged with standard piano size keys or smaller piano accordion size keys. If you already play the piano, or hold this as a goal, purchase one with the large keys. The smaller keys are quite adequate if you do not feel any need to match up to existing conventions.

Piano

It is possible to adopt a 'guitar like' style for piano accompaniment work by combining the ideas previously described for other instruments. Imagine a 'player cake' as a model for the musical events required to produce a pleasing overall musical effect for accompanying singing. The melody/tune is the most important part of the overall sound, with a bass part to act as a harmonic foundation and chords to fill out the middle section. Rhythm is also used to provide lift and pace. In the absence of percussion instruments, a combination of bass and chord playing accomplishes this rhythmic role.

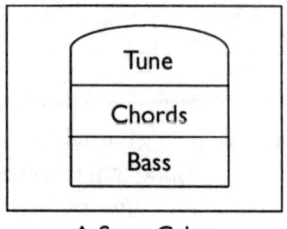

A Song Cake

Looking at a song in this way permits a new division of labour. If the top is left to the singer, only the middle and bass parts remain the accompaniment players' domain. This middle/bass playing can be reduced by adopting the following pattern playing technique. Begin to develop a style which is based on a pattern playing principle, involving the rhythmic division of chords and bass. Immediately we relinquish reading complex notation, using the additional mental space to focus on a stronger rhythmic and harmonic content. The techniques operate in this way:

Right Hand

Begin by looking through the song to find the required chords; use the guitar chords printed in the music to work out this information. For the sake of this exercise the chords could be **C, F, G, Am** and **Em**. We need to know which notes are required in the chord. (See Appendix 3.) Playing these chord notes forms the shape of events in the right hand.

Left Hand

The left hand bass notes can be calculated by looking again at the notes in the chord. The notes in the chosen chords are:

Chord			C	F	G	Am	Em
		5	g	c	d	e	b
Notes		3	e	a	b	c	g
		1	c	f	g	a	e

For each chord we use notes 1 and 5 alternating in the bass. Start on note 1.

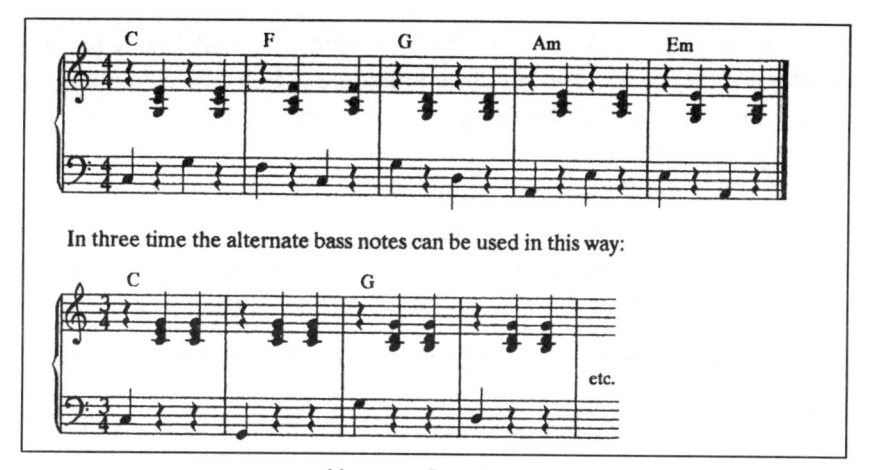

[Musical notation: Chord progression C, F, G, Am, Em with alternate bass notes]

In three time the alternate bass notes can be used in this way:

[Musical notation: C and G chords in 3/4 time]

Alternate Bass Notes

The chord notes and shapes used in a piece should be firmly in your memory before attempting to accompany a song. Once you know how to play the chords, the mental and physical demand is to play the appropriate chord and bass pattern almost as a reflex action. In turn this is related to the chord symbols written above the song words. This is a less complex cerebral demand then reading a full piano part. Your technique will improve as you gain in experience and fluency.

Rhythmic Style

Listen to the way the auto-chord system of a keyboard derives bass and chords using regular patterns. Copy the flavour used to rhythmically divide bass and chords in these instruments. This is a technique for extending your range of styles. In particular a Latin-American style is extremely useful (123,123,12). The notation appears a little intimidating at first but stay with it! Work at it by playing alongside a keyboard rhythm section (rhumba, bossa nova. Speed 130).

[Musical notation: C chord in Latin-American rhythm]

Latin-American Rhythm

Accompaniments devised in this way tend to sound best when the chords are played in positions close to middle c. Remember to minimise finger movements when changing from one chord to the next.

Chords with a 7th

Any chords with symbols including numbers (C7) possess one additional note to the three we already know about. The following simple rules will explain the knowledge required to add a 7th to a chord when required:

- The additional note is always two semi-tones lower than note 1 of the chord.
- Leave note 1 out of the right hand part and replace it with the 7th.
- The 7th will sound best in the middle of the cluster of notes played.

Notes of the music scale form a repeating pattern, notes 1 and 8 having the same name:

```
c d e f g a b c
1 2 3 4 5 6 7 8
```

The 7th is the seventh note of the scale. This seventh note then needs to be flattened in order to give the required aural effect (b♭).

Breaking up the Chord Notes

Notes of a chord can be broken up into different patterns to achieve a

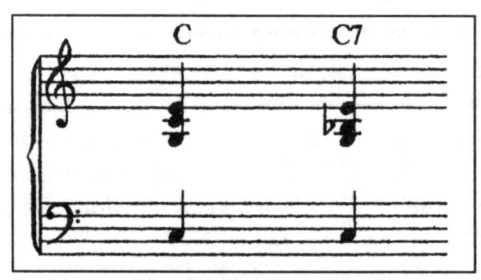

C and C7 Chords

variety of movements (feel). As you develop different styles, several of them can be used within the same accompaniment. Continuing to use the chord of C, styles could follow these examples:

Flowing Style

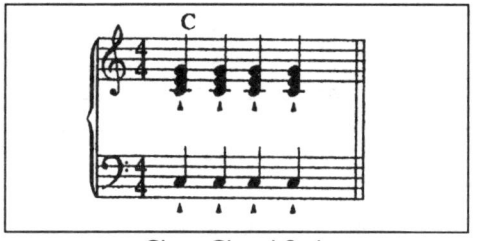

Chop Chord Style

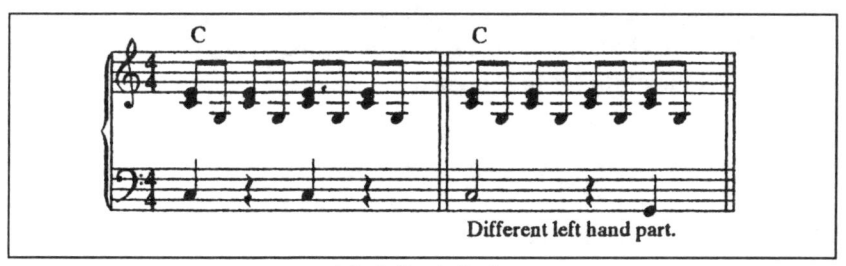

Mod. Rock Style

Introductions and Links

Play firm introductions and link passages between verses. The most obvious of introductions leads the singer's ear to the keynote of the song. Playing five notes of a descending scale will achieve a basic introduction. Add some of the chord notes to fill out the sound. This strategy can be used as an introduction to most of your songs.

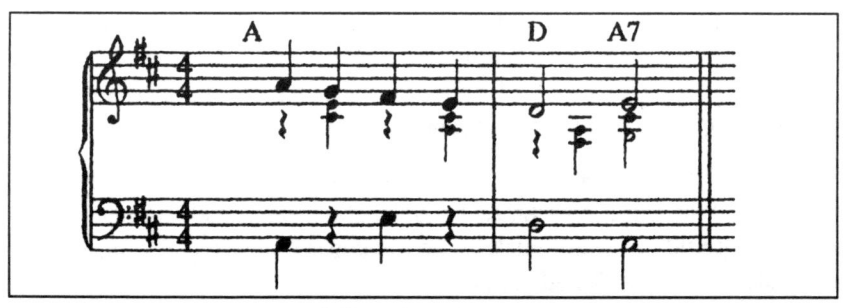

A Basic Introduction

Introduction and song should be played at the same speed. Singers are required to 'catch' the pulse during this short snippet; therefore, avoid speed changes and pauses. The last few bars of a tune provide another way of devising a suitable introduction, this strategy reminding the singer of the tune:

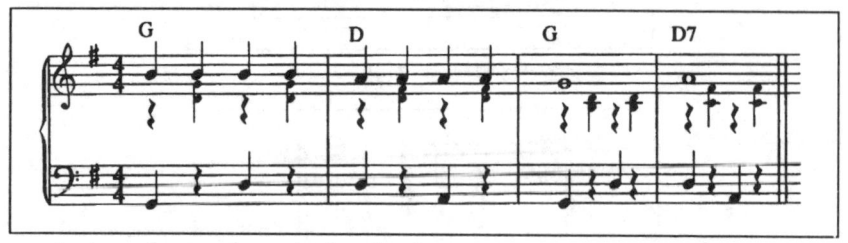

An Introduction from the last few bars

1, 2 or 4 bars from the end of a song serve
as an introduction. Add the chord V7 if you
wish to add a stronger feeling of leading back to the beginning.

Similar musical ideas can be used to link verses together to maintain a feeling of momentum for the singers.

Guitar

The guitar is a very popular instrument for accompaniment playing. It possesses a tremendous amount of credibility with young people and is conveniently portable. It is an instrument requiring several months of dedication for initially establishing basic skills. Some of the following ideas will assist in smoothing out the process.

- Left hand fingers require strength and hard skin on the pads. This is achieved by playing little and often; there is a slight pain barrier to work through. Classical guitars with nylon strings are gentler on the fingers than the steel strings of a folk instrument.
- Spend a little time adjusting the action of your guitar. Look along the length of the strings to see if the neck of the instrument is flat and level. If the neck is bowed the instrument will be quite difficult to play even in the most experienced of hands. Bowed necks cannot be rectified, they have to be lived with. Second-hand buyers beware!

Place the guitar on a table and look at the instrument from the side. From this view examine the distance between the strings and the neck. This distance should be approximately the thickness of a two pence piece. If it is greater then consider adjustment by:

i) Lowering the height of the bridge. Some folk guitars have adjusting screws built into the bridge. Alternatively the bridge will have a white plastic piece which can be removed and sanded down.

ii) A plastic piece (end nut) at the head of the instrument can have the depth of grooves slightly increased by using a fine hacksaw blade or file. Replacement plastic pieces are readily available from music shops should you damage or overadjust either piece. To deepen the grooves, slacken off the tension from one string at a time, work on the plastic groove and then re-tension the string. Check the result and move on to the next. Fine gauge strings can be adjusted closer to the neck. If the bass strings are too close they will buzz and rattle.

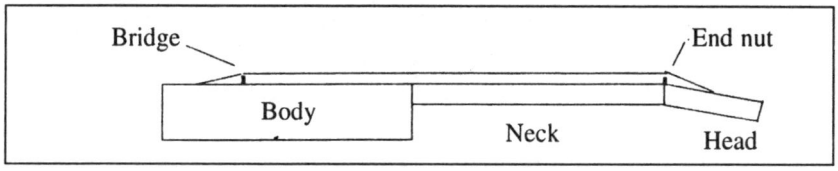

Adjusting the action

Chord Shapes

Guitar players quickly realise how two or three chords can be used to strum an effective accompaniment to a song. Players learn chord shapes; very often the chord is played without any knowledge of the individual notes involved. This shape information could well be processed by a different area of the brain. It clearly is a simple way of storing complex information.

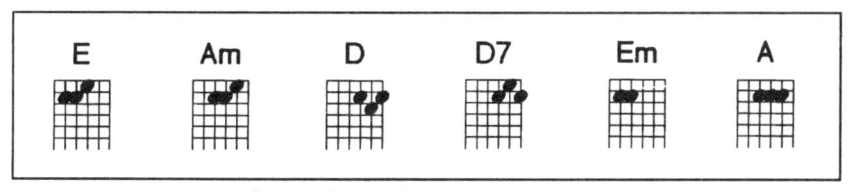

Three Guitar Chord Visual Shapes

A mirror image of the letter L, a triangle and a horizontal line are represented in the six chords illustrated. Usually one finger takes the lead and the other fingers fall into the shape behind it. **A, D & E** are good chords to become familiar with initially. They all have different shapes. Try this pattern:

| A / / / | D / / / | A / / / | E / / / |

| A / / / | D / / / | E / D / | A / / / |

With a fluent repertoire of these three chords, useful guitar work can quickly be incorporated into the accompaniment of many songs.

Feeling the Pinch

Become aware of the way a guitar is sometimes fulfilling the role of a rhythmic instrument that is only partly achieved by strumming. A squeezing action can be adopted in the left hand, timed to be part of the musical pulse. Experiment by holding down a chord and then using a squeeze on the beat and relaxing in between. The chord should have a clean sound when the pressure is applied and a woolly rhythmic quality during the relaxed part. Experiment with relaxing some or all of the fingers in this technique. The squeezing makes it easier to sustain continued playing. As you progress, it will also extend the period of playing time before the hand becomes totally fatigued. Experiment to develop your own rhythmic feels and styles.

The Capo

A device which helps to make a few guitar chord shapes go a long way. It fixes round the neck at any point and effectively becomes a movable end nut. There are several clever designs of capo to try out at your local music shop. If the capo is fixed across the first fret, play the chord shape of **A**; it will sound as a **B♭**. All the chords played will be a semitone higher. Fix the capo across the second fret and all the chords then become a tone higher, and so on up the neck. Using a capo in this way makes it easy to play a song in a higher or lower key. Tuning becomes more critical the higher up the neck a capo is positioned. Folk players enjoy using a capo because of the characteristic twang made by the shorter strings, a preferred tonal quality for some music.

	I	IV	V
Normal Chord Shape	A	D	E
Fret 1	B♭	E♭	F
Fret 2	B	E	F♯
Capo across fret 3	C	F	G
Fret 4	C♯	F♯	G♯
Capo across fret 5	D	G	A

Capo Chords

Transposing (For All Instruments)

Moving a tune or a chord sequence up or down is known as transposing. This chart will allow you to read off the information required to achieve this technique. (Moving up the chart = higher, down the chart = lower.) The chart is not exhaustive and is a little biased towards guitar players.

Key	Notes of the scale.							
A (3♯'s)	a	b	c♯	d	e	f♯	g♯	a
G (1♯)	g	a	b	c	d	e	f♯	g
F (1♭)	f	g	a	b♭	c	e	e	f
E (4♯'s)	e	f♯	g♯	a	b	c♯	d♯	e
D (2♯'s)	d	e	f♯	g	a	b	c♯	d
C	d	e	f	g	a	b	c	
B (5♯'s)	b	c♯	d♯	e	f♯	g♯	a♯	b
A (3♯'s)	a	b	c♯	d	e	f♯	g♯	a
Chord Numbers	I	II	III	IV	V	VI	VII	VIII

Transposition Chart

If you are playing the accompaniment to a song in **A** (3♯s) using the chords of **A, D & E** and wish to make the song higher, follow the chords up to a new horizontal line and read off the new chords. If we move up two rows, the new chords are **C, F & G**. The new key is **C**. Notes of a tune are transposed by the same process. Because of the repeating pattern of ascending/descending music notes, the chart simply repeats to go higher or lower.

CHAPTER 8

Organisation and Resources to Make Music Special

The Time and Place

When and where the activities take place require serious consideration. Music making is a noisy pursuit. Musical concepts are acquired by the making and shaping of our own music. It becomes our duty to establish the most conducive climate for promoting the subject in this way. Take a look at areas used for art. All around there will be evidence of artistic fallout, fragments of visual art material which somehow failed to land where the artist wished (paint and water split on the floor etc.). All this splatter occurs and is handled in a natural fashion, part of realistic expectations and evidence of work taking place. Creating music has an aural fall-out which we should equally expect and permit. Expect young people to spill sound in their attempts to accurately place it! Some readers will have specialist purpose-built rooms, whilst others work in a variety of locations including open plan environments. Not all neighbours or colleagues are likely to share our musical enlightenment. Our noisy rivalry cannot always be considered as fair.

At a minimum base level, we need to negotiate with colleagues and plan ahead. Different times of the day can be set aside for noise making, whilst other times are quiet. There will always be creative solutions to finding times and places for music to occur. The resolution to problems will, of necessity, be particular to your own environment. An ideal should encompass:

- Access to a wide choice of instruments at all times of the day.
- Locations which are conducive to the activity taking place.

- Areas under easy supervision.
- Places where sound can happen without disturbance to others.

Some of us will have to compromise these factors and in some way reduce our opportunities for flexibility and access. That is life! Other choices include a music corner, the touring music trolley, the hall, a handy corridor or the specialised activity room. Some of these are poor options, but many teachers produce quality work without access to particularly conducive locations.

Silence

There will always be times when silence is required, both to appreciate its quality and also for it to become a vessel into which we place our music. Settle for a few moments of silence as a minimum before a piece is performed. Total silence is virtually an abstract commodity nowadays, but do avoid unwanted sounds in compositions. They quickly kill the creative atmosphere and reduce the level of sensitivity. (Talking, fiddling with instruments and coughing are the most common offenders.) The careful use of dynamics, in a relative sense, is to be recommended. Maximum volume levels in a shared work area should be quieter than maximum volume in a remote location. (A question of, 'What is loud music?' and What is quiet music?') Young people produce excellent work at low volume levels. Pausing and punctuating sessions with a song or another musical activity can be a way of pulling back instrumental volume. Noise has a tendency to gradually increase over time.

There are some music legacies which do not serve us well. Historically large groups have enjoyed singing, so people think all musical activities cater for similar sized groups. This is a myth. Consider ways of dividing into small groups for practical work. It is possible to engage larger groups in a broad range of activities where music may be included.

Music sessions should be as frequent as possible. When approaching the subject from a philosophical stance, describing music as basic communication, to not provide access is to inhibit expression. Utopia is for music to become an option alongside all other work topics, throughout the day Sometimes music-related exercises masquerade as other things (sequencing, patterns, rhymes). Anyone working from a topic-based approach could consider placing musical ideas as the focus of a topic instead of in a supporting role. Creative thinking will acknowledge the allocation of quality time for our subject within the context of crowded study programmes. Music is not a final tag on or afterthought.

Instrument Resources

Practical music will always involve the use of percussion instruments in some way. This will necessitate the continual extension and improvement of resources. All the equipment should be in a good state of repair, clean, appealing and varied. Students at an early stage of development, with only gross motor control skills, require controllable instruments. Thin handles, narrow bars and instruments requiring a difficult level of physical dexterity, should be avoided. There is abundant evidence to indicate the results of short-term purchasing policies. Too many triangles, castanets, tambourines (some with an acute hernia!), claves and other cheap instruments abound. It seems as if they quietly reproduce in the dark depths of music trolleys! Maracas and guiros are of exceptional quality if they survive a year of intensive use. Expect to replace them.

Each year we should aim to buy at least one quality instrument which will both last and excite our players. Aim to visit your instrument supplier, have a go on instruments you are interested in. Any two with identical appearances can sound completely different. You may prefer the sound of one to another. Pictures in catalogues will not give you such aural information. In round terms, a basic stock of equipment requires instruments in sufficient quantities, which are easily played and present a variety of choice for the young players. A leaning towards un-tuned percussion is likely in the earlier stages. As we progress the work demands a greater involvement in musical pitch, hence a need for more tuned instruments.

The ability to remove and move bars around on tuned percussion instruments permits an analytical approach for developing our understanding of melody and harmony. This is the equivalent of showing 'working out' in a complex equation. It is concrete operational in nature, not so abstract. This is very desirable. The sophistication of high quality expensive instruments will continually taunt us all. Acquire the finest selection possible.

Collecting Sounds

Sound sources surround us. They do not have to be particularly expensive to intrigue young people. Collections of sounds produced from everyday items can readily be accumulated. Three ornaments, four assorted plastic containers and two stones could be quite sufficient to provide the accompaniment for a poem. Novelty value has always played a part in music. Our search for unique sounds and ways of controlling them has provided the motivation for every instrumental invention. We can recycle, hunt out, invent and re-think many objects into our musical compositions. What can you do with a few sheets of newspaper? Some scientific knowledge can expand this further.

Instruments and Science

Th science of sound has many implications for musicians. Although it is a detailed subject in its own right, some knowledge will help if we wish to develop the use of environmental sounds or make our own instruments. Existing instruments have long established scientific principles, governing shape, tonal quality, pitch, volume and so on. They have evolved over long periods of time.

Try this experiment with a pair of claves. We are presented with two pieces of dark red wood approximately 18 cm long and 2 cm in diameter. Hold the claves tightly and hit them together; they make a sound, but it will be fairly dull and dead. If we cradle one clave across a closed hand and hold the other lightly about 3 cm from the end, the sound produced is resonant, bright and interesting. Careful handling of the wood permits greater resonance. The musical tone and pitch are improved. Hold each clave in different places to find where the location of this 'sweet spot' is. When exploring everyday objects, a trial and error method is the best way of finding this place.

The 'sweet spot' for items of a regular shape is easy to calculate. Examine our pair of claves again. The optimum place for holding them is roughly between a quarter and a fifth of their length, from either end. This point has the least musical activity, it is common to all bars and tubes and is extremely important when exploring sound sources. The xylophone, glockenspiel and tubular bells all rely on this phenomenon for their design and construction. The measurements can be closely approximated.

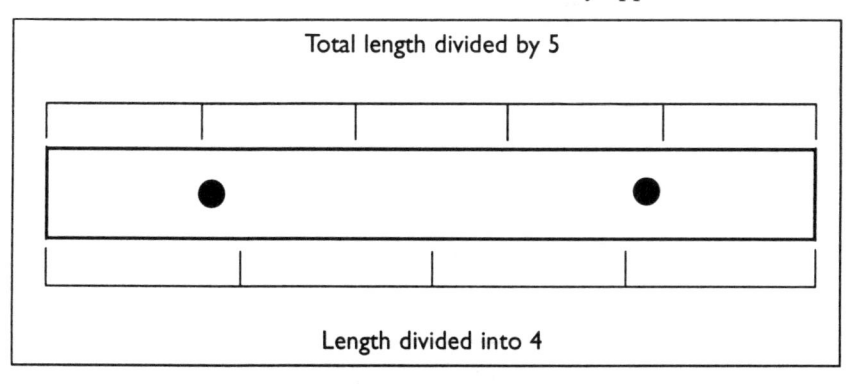

The 'Sweet Spot'

These 'sweet spots' are scientifically termed 'nodes'. With this knowledge, continue to experiment by listening to objects held at a node position (ruler, rolling pin, pencil, solid steel cutlery).

Making a Xylophone

Using the node information it becomes straightforward to make your own 'tuned' percussion instruments in this way. Buy a 2 m length of dowel (approximately 3 cm diameter) or a sweeping brush handle. Cut the wood into different lengths. Start with a 20 cm piece and make each consecutive piece approximately 4 to 5 cm longer. Taking each piece in turn, measure its length and, using a calculator, multiply the length of the wood by 0.225. This will give you the measurement for the node (20 cm multiplied by 0.225 = 4.5 cm). Measure the answer to your calculation from either end of the wood and make a pencil mark to indicate the position of the nodes. Roll out some plasticine into a long sausage and place short lengths where the the nodes are marked. The plasticine will support the wood clear of the table and prevent it from rolling around. In the illustration below the plasticine corresponds to the string. Play these wooden bars with a hard beater.

If you have access to more tools and wish to spend additional time, drill holes at the nodes and string the bars together. Use knots in the string or short lengths of clear plastic tube (windscreen washer pipe) to provide spacers between each note.

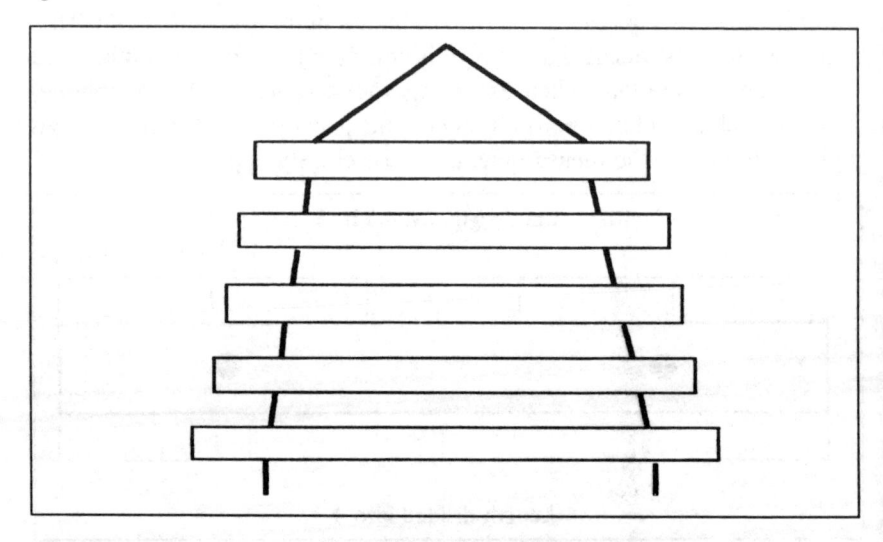

Home-Made Xylophone

This horizontal arrangement is good for relating pitch to height. The longest bar has the lowest pitch and the shortest has the highest note. The specific pitch of each note will be random. Accept it as a loosely tuned instrument. (Density, diameter and type of material also affect the pitch.)

Bells

The same design can be successfully employed using different materials for the bars: thick bamboo cane (ask at the carpet shop, some carpets are rolled onto cane), dowel of different diameter, different types of wood, metal tubing such as 22 mm copper pipe or recycle metal tubing from vacuum cleaner tools. A variation is to suspend the bars vertically from one node using string or cord. Perhaps the lowest note would be in the region of 1 metre in length – the choice is yours:

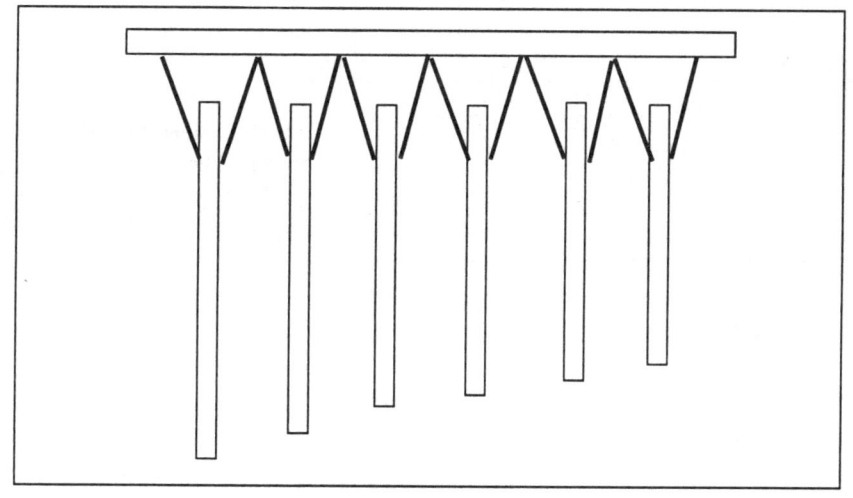

Home-Made Tubular Bells

These plans are scientific starting points, each idea will require a specific design by the young people. Plans naturally develop during the construction stages. Frames, number of bars, length, materials, decoration and so on all require careful thought.

If you wish to think big this idea will work for large tubular bells constructed from scaffolding tube. This is ideal for musical playgrounds.

Chimes

Chimes are made along similar lines and can be made from wood, shell, metal bar or tube. A set of percussive chimes can be constructed for a small amount of money. Start by consulting the yellow pages to locate a supplier of aluminium bar (4 mm to 5 mm in diameter). Cut the first note to be 20 cm long and progress by cutting further lengths, making each one approximately 5 mm shorter. This will consume between 3.5 m and 4 m of material. Because of the relatively short length of the notes the difference between node points becomes insignificant. This makes it reasonable to drill a hole through every note in a similar place. (Between 1.5 cm and 2.5 cm works satisfactorily.) A hacksaw, electric drill, suitable work area and attention to safety are required. Nylon kite string should be used to lace the instrument together using a 'V' shape to hold each bar away from the next.

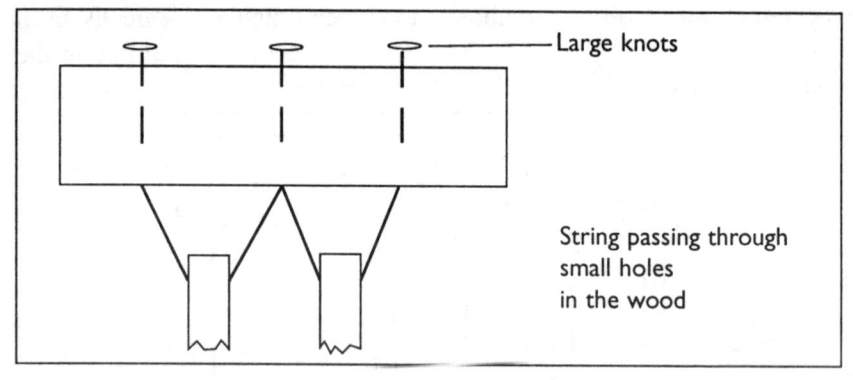

Lacing together

Wind Chimes

Wind chimes (see p.119) are constructed by placing the bars in a circular shape. (Star, hexagon or other regular shapes can be used.) If the instrument is to live outside, use leather boot laces for the stringing. To enable the wind to 'play' the instrument a wooden bead is fixed to a central lace; the bead should be approximately 2 cm away from each chime. Attach a piece of wood, plastic or aluminium about the size of a playing card to act as a small sail at the end of the centre bead clapper. The amount of wind required is related to the distance between the bead and the chimes, the size of the sail and the weight of material used.

Drum Making

Drums are popular instruments to make. The skin exerts considerable force in all directions demanding a shape which is capable of withstanding high tension. Drum heads must be taut if the instrument is to

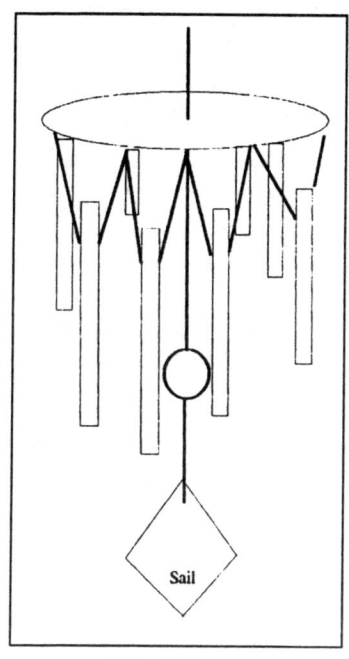

Wind Power

produce a satisfying sound. Applying tension is not easy. Drums with animal skin rely on the natural expansion and contraction qualities of the skin to exert this tension. Real skin is applied after a thorough soaking. It is nailed or bound to a shell and becomes exceptionally tight as the skin dries out. If you have any drums with loose heads, wet the skin with warm water whilst still on the drum and then leave it to dry out. African drummers sometimes face their drum heads towards open fires to achieve rapid drying. Many drums of modern design use plastic imitation skin which does not have any natural shrinking properties. These drums require mechanical means to apply tension.

Effective home-made instruments can be developed by laminating layers of fabric soaked in white PVA glue over the top of cardboard tubes or plastic buckets; 20 cm to 25 cm is the maximum diameter for drums made in this way. The construction involves cutting out fabric scraps, soaking them in the glue and then spreading the pieces over the top of the drum body and down the sides. Several layers provide a good strong finish. It is important to ensure that each piece of fabric is large enough to extend well down the sides of the drum. Slit the material down the sides to reduce folds. Before leaving the drum to dry out check that the head is smooth and taut.

Drums constructed from cardboard tubes produce different tonal qualities in relationship to the lengths used – long for low, short for high.

Fabric Pattern

Try making a pair of drums, one 50 cm and another 70 cm. Play these drums adopting a bongo playing style. Generally drum sticks will drastically reduce the life of home-made drums. (Drum sticks drastically reduce the life of all drums!) Read on for a source of free cardboard tube.

Booming Bass Notes

This home-made instrument produces low bass notes for very little cost. Ask a carpet fitter for the tube carpets are rolled on. This could be cardboard or, better still, plastic. (Plastic drain pipe can also be purchased from the local DIY shop. Try out the sound next time you wish to brighten up a visit to the local branch of Texiwixihomibyandquietalli Super Store.) Start with a very long piece, about 3 m. Cut several more pieces, progressively making each one shorter. (Cut with a wood saw.) Lay them side by side on the floor with ends lined up and a generous space between each one.

Measure the distance from side to side and procure two pieces of wood cut to the measured length. Drill holes in the wood large enough for washing line to pass through. Lash the tubes together to hold the structure firm. This large instrument requires a pair of special beaters made from high density foam. A yoga mat or lightweight camping roll are suitable. Stick several layers together and cut into a table tennis bat shape. The

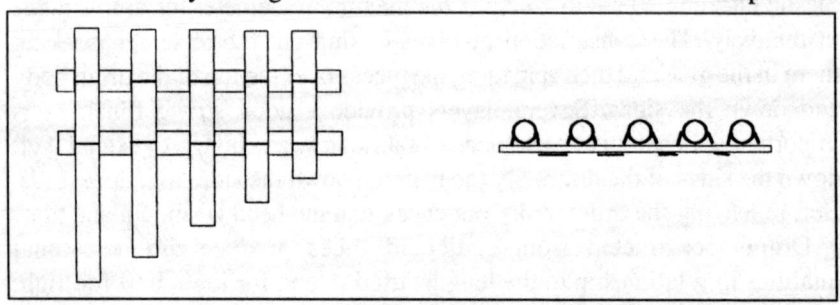

Lashing Down

tubes are played by 'plopping' the foam over the open end of the tubes. The result is a rich satisfying sound.

Presentation and Pitch

All home-made instruments require an amount of experimentation to complete their design. This provides a proportion of the fun in making things with young people and is integral to the learning experience. Initially you could make one pipe or even two for drone playing. The instruments become more original by hand painting patterns and designs.

Bass pipes and chimes are not tuned to any specific notes in this method of construction. Spend time cutting off small pieces of each pipe if you wish to specifically tune them. Each time a section of pipe is removed the pitch will be slightly higher Match up the pitch of the notes you require from another instrument or use an electronic tuner. Start with the lowest note you require. If you cut too much tube away then work on to make it the next lowest note. It will take time and care to achieve accurate tuning.

Un-tuned Tuned Percussion

The tuning of scales has evolved over hundreds of years. It is based on a scientific compromise and has become standardised. This standardisation has established the ground rules for harmonic theory. When instruments have a random tuning they immediately stand outside all the conventional rules associated with Western music and require a different set of ground rules for making music. Here are some possible suggestions to explore:

- Use a strong rhythmic content in the music.
- Try playing different patterns of notes – some patterns will be more satisfying. Discover the patterns by trial and error.
- Build up the music by having one pattern on top of another (layered ostinati) and modify existing patterns in relationship to the new pattern.
- Use dynamics to focus on lead parts and/or accompaniments.
- Allow players to be influenced by the other musical events happening within the composition (changes of speed, rhythm pattern and so on).
- Trust your ears to be the final judge.
- Recognise the mysterious beauty encapsulated within music based on these techniques and using primitive instruments.

Do not forget about shakers and scrapers, they are very simple to make and hold equally important roles for music making with our young people. Their design is straightforward and obvious.

Appendix 1

The Relationship of Notes in Musical Scales

Conventional music notation tends to make the space between notes appear to be the same distance. As you can see from these illustrations they are quite different. The word 'scale' comes from the Latin word *scala* which means a flight of steps, stairs or a ladder. These illustrations compare major, minor and whole-tone scales with the equal steps of a chromatic scale:

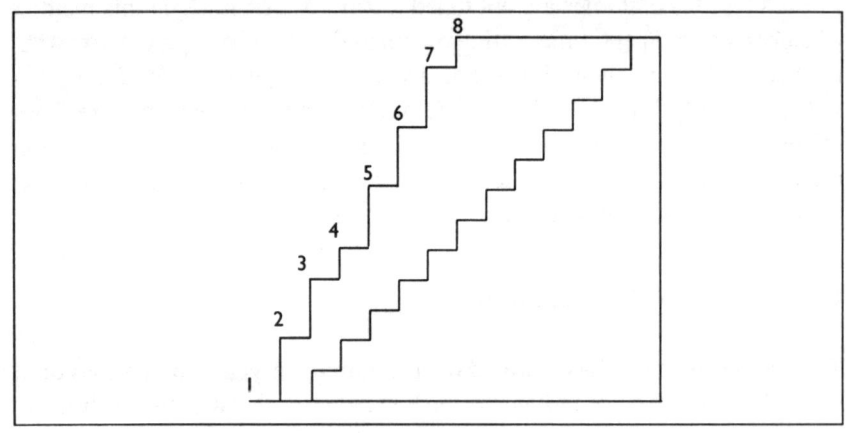

The Major Scale

Numbers are used here because scales can start on any note. The spacing between each note remains constant for each type of scale, irrespective of starting note. There are several varieties of minor scale. This is an example of a harmonic minor scale.

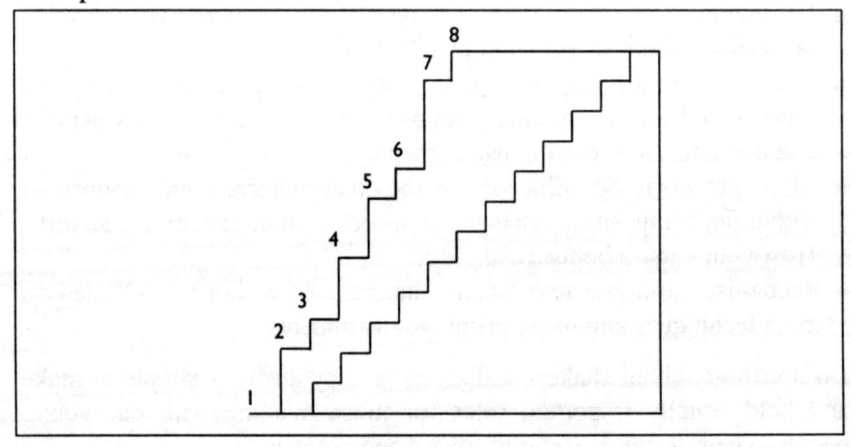

The Harmonic Minor Scale

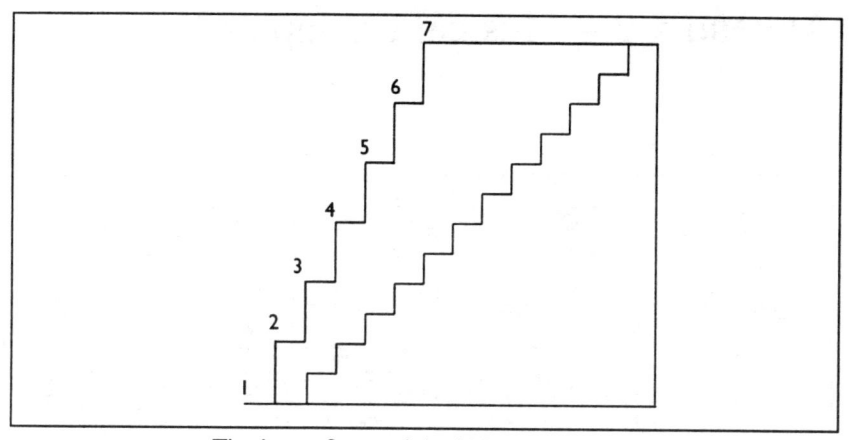

The Large Steps of the Whole-tone Scale

Modes

The Dorian and Aeolian modes are useful for improvising. Both modes have seven different notes with a different order of spacing between them. The modes are shown starting on **d** and **a** respectively. They can, and often do, start on any other note. These are good versions to begin with.

d e - f g a b - c d

Notes of the Dorian Mode

a b - c d e - f g a

Notes of the Aeolian Mode

The staircase for each mode possesses a different spacing between each ascending note. Draw them out on graph paper if you require an illustration. The significant factors are the location of tone and semitone spaces between notes.

Appendix 2 – Musical Examples

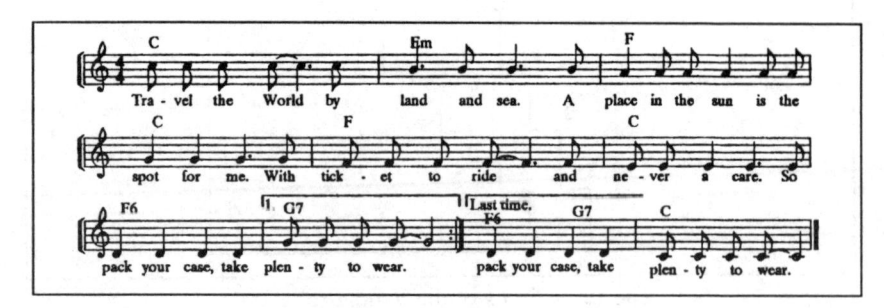

Tra-vel the World by land and sea. A place in the sun is the spot for me. With tick-et to ride and ne-ver a care. So pack your case, take plen-ty to wear. pack your case, take plen-ty to wear.

What Makes A Cake?

Hey! Ho! What makes a cake?
Sugar with spice and all things nice.
Marzipan and icing on the top.

>Hey! Ho! Let's bake a cake!
>Hey! Ho! With butter and sugar.
>Marzipan and icing on the top.

Hey! Ho! Crack in the eggs.
Hey! Ho! Shake in the flour.
Marzipan and icing on the top.

>Hey! Ho! Sprinkle in the currants.
>Hey! Ho! Throw in the nuts.
>Marzipan and icing on the top.

Hey! Ho! It's all in the bowl.
Hey! Ho! Mix it round.
Marzipan and icing on the top.

>Hey! Ho! Put it in a tin.
>Hey! Ho! Take it to the oven.
>Marzipan and icing on the top.

Hey! Ho! We've made a cake!
Sugar and spice and all things nice.
Marzipan and icing on the top.

What Makes A Cake?

Hey! Ho! What makes a cake? [repeat] Su-gar with spice and all things nice. [repeat] Mar-zi-pan with i-cing on the top.

Appendix 3

Common Chords

I.	C major	c	e	g				C
II.	D minor	d	f	a				Dm
III.	E minor		e	g	b			Em
IV.	F major			f	a	c		F
V.	G major				g	b	d	G
VI.	A minor				a	c	e	Am
VII.	B diminished				b	d	f	Bdim.

The left hand note should be the lowest note played

Chords

The lowest note (LH) is used for naming a chord. Someone talking about a chord of **C** is referring to the notes (**c, e** and **g**) played together. Numbers are also employed. (The convention is to use roman numerals.) The roman numeral system has implications related to scales. Chord **I** is a chord built on the first note of a scale, chord **II** is a chord built on the second note of the scale and so on.

The diagram also illustrates chords of three different types – major, minor and diminished. Each has a distinguishing aural flavour. The difference between the three types of chord is achieved by changing the musical distance between the three notes.

Spare Bars

Most tuned percussion instruments are supplied with a number of spare bars – f♯ c♯ and b♭. These notes will enable you to work with the following chords:

D major	d		f♯		a					D
A major					a		c♯		e	A
B♭ major						b♭		d		f	B♭
G minor				g		b♭		d		Gm

Chords Using f♯, c♯ and b♭

Keyboards and chromatic tuned percussion have many more chords available.

The difference between major and minor chords is established by examining the middle note of the chord. Lowering the middle note of a major chord by a semitone results in a minor chord.

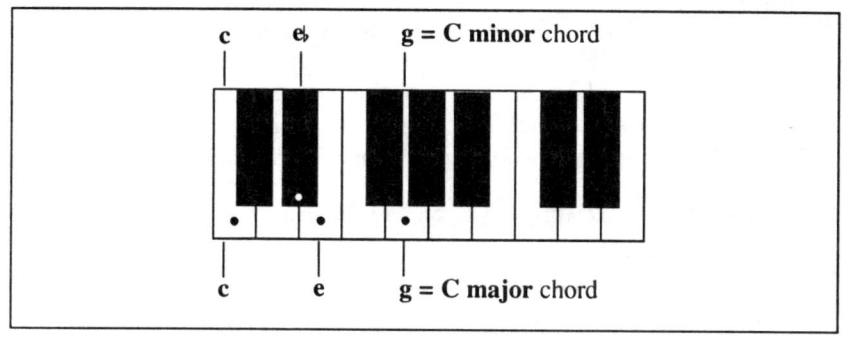

c   e♭   g = **C minor** chord

c   e   g = **C major** chord

The reverse is also true. Raising the middle note of a minor chord by a semitone results in a major chord. If further help is required, search in the back pages of keyboard music books to discover pictures of other chords. It is common to shuffle the order of notes in a chord. **e, g, c** and **g, c, e** remain the chord of C major.

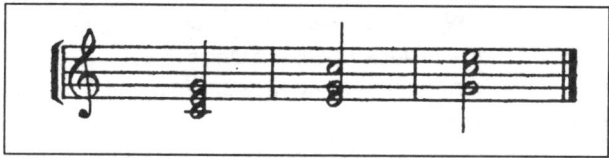

Different Positions of Chords

The different notes in a chord can be used any number of times.

Repeating Notes in a Chord

Further Reading

Appleby, A. and Pickow, P. (1992) *The Songwriter's Companion*. New York: Amsco.
Baxter, K. (1980) *Play the Chromaharp*. Nottingham: Kate Baxter, PO Box 149, Nottingham, NG3 5PU.
Baxter, K. (1994) *Fundamental Activities*. Nottingham: Fundamental Activities.
Bennett, R. (1990) *Music Dictionary*. Harlow: Longman.
Binns, T. (1994) *Children Making Music*. Hemel Hempstead: Simon & Schuster Education.
Birkenshaw, L. (1974) *Music For Fun, Music For Learning*. Toronto: Holt, Rinehart & Winston.
Blom, E. (1962) *Everyman's Dictionary of Music*. London: Dent.
Bloomfield, A. (1985) *Creative and Aesthetic Education*. Hull: University of Hull.
Campbell, I. (1969) *Come Listen*. London: Ginn.
DfE (1995) *Music in the National Curriculum*. London: HMSO.
Farmer, B. (1982) *Springboards*. Melbourne: Nelson.
Gilbert, G. (1981) *Musical Starting Points with Young Children*. East Grinstead: Ward Lock Educational.
Green, B. and Gallwey, W. T. *The Inner Game of Music*. London: Pan Books.
Grigson, L. (1988) *Practical Jazz*. London: Stainer & Bell.
Gross, R. D. (1993) *Psychology: The Science of Mind and Behaviour*. London: Hodder & Stoughton.
Johnston, I. (1989) *Measured Tones*. Bristol: Institute of Physics Publishing.
Kennedy, M. (1980) *The Concise Oxford Dictionary of Music*. Oxford: Oxford University Press.
McNicol, R. (1992) *Sound Inventions*. Oxford: Oxford University Press.
Meyer-Denkmann, G. (1977) *Experiments in Sound*. London: Universal.
Mills, J. (1991) *Music in the Primary School*. Cambridge: Cambridge University Press.
Osborne, N. (1989) *Musical Projects and Games*. Woodford Green: International Music.
Rolla, M. G. (1993) *Your Inner Music*. Wilmette, Illinois: Chiron Publications.
Storr, A. (1986) *The Dynamics of Creation*. Harmondsworth: Pelican/Penguin Books.
Sylva, K. and Lunt, I. (1986) *Child Development*. Oxford: Blackwell.
Thorne, B. (1992) *Carl Rogers*. London: Sage.
Walker, J. (1983) *The Rhyming Dictionary*. London: Routledge & Kegan Paul.

Index

accompaniment/s 5, 37, 43, 60–1, 100–108, 121
actions/movement 13, 22, 77
African rhythms 29
art form/s 86, 87, 88
autism/autistic 72

bass drum 84
bass notes 101, 120
bass parts 104–108
bass sounds 18
bass xylophone 72, 85
beaters 12, 46, 67, 73, 121
binary form 22
blues 23, 54

capo 109–10
chant 27, 29–30
chord sequences 58, 79, 95, 110
chordal zithers 99–100
chords 24, 38–44, 49–54, 59, 61–3, 65, 74, 93, 96, 99–108, 109–11
chromaharp 99
communication 70, 71, 72, 85, 113
concert pitch 60
conducting 11
conversation 4, 24, 31, 55, 86, 99
copying 72, 76, 77, 89
creative focus 89
creativity 86, 98
crotchet 55

drones 34–8
drums 59
dynamics 85, 121

echo clapping 30, 61
eighth notes 55
emotions 1, 69, 72, 80, 89

flat/s 26, 58, 106
form 6, 20–2

glockenspiel 18, 51, 57, 60, 65, 115
graphic notation 33
greeting song 83–4
guitar 27, 42, 46, 47, 51, 60, 65, 78, 79, 85, 104, 108–11

half note 55
hearing 9, 17, 23, 70

imagination 23, 75, 85, 86, 97
imaginative play 87
imitation 5, 72
intelligence 69, 78, 86, 87–8
inter-personal relationships 82
introductions 102, 107

keyboard 9, 14, 17, 24, 26, 36, 48, 51, 57, 59, 60, 61–3, 65–6, 79, 96, 100, 102–17

language 1, 2–4, 11, 31, 69, 71, 72, 73, 75, 83, 85
Latin-American rhythm 29, 38, 81, 105
learning 2–4, 9, 69, 79, 83, 87, 97, 99, 121
learning difficulties 2, 3, 69–85
learning model 81
leitmotiv 91
link passages 107
listening 2, 5, 13, 22–3, 47, 65, 76, 80, 116

MIDI 65–8
major chords 41–2, 51–2, 100, 101, 102–105
major scale 53, 57–8
measures 27
media 8–9, 63, 89
metre 28, 54, 59, 95
metronome 14
microphone 46–7, 48–9, 64, 67
minim 55
minor chords 41–2, 52, 63, 100
mirroring 72

modes 59–60, 79
mood 10, 20, 22, 27, 59, 73, 99
mood music 90
motor control 7, 71, 118
music ingredients 5–8, 14, 20, 22, 24, 93
music therapy 84
musical development 3, 6–7, 74, 90, 102

National Curriculum 4
nodes 115–6
notation 5, 31–4, 54–8, 99, 103, 105

observation 89
ostinati/o 39–40, 47, 85, 121
overture 91

pentatonic scale 24–5, 35–7, 39, 43, 57, 60, 72, 73
personal development 1–3, 69, 79, 82
piano 12, 17, 20, 38, 47, 52, 61, 65, 71, 73, 79, 85, 93, 103–108
piano accordion 28, 100–2, 104
pitch 9–7, 17–20, 22, 24, 26–7, 33, 34, 45, 54, 56–7, 64, 71, 72, 76, 93, 114, 117, 121
progression 1, 4–6, 33, 45
pulse 13–14, 16, 21, 28–30, 35, 37, 38, 40, 42, 55, 59, 73, 89, 108
puppets 75–6

quarter note 55
quaver 55

rapping 62
recitative 91
recording 47–48
recording – multi-track 63–5, 68
resources 9, 46, 112–5
rhythm 6, 13, 16–7, 29–31, 33, 54, 59, 90, 93, 105
rhythmic style 22, 105
riffs 49–53
role models 2, 89

rondo 21, 91

scales 24, 27, 57–60, 122–3
science 115
semibreve 55
senses 9, 13, 18
sharps 26, 58
silence 32, 113
singing 5, 30, 36, 37, 48, 76–7, 99, 113
skills 2, 5, 7, 12, 33, 56, 67, 69, 76, 91, 99, 101, 114
song/s 21, 37–44, 49–51, 53, 76–78, 80, 83, 95–98, 100, 104
sound pictures 94
speech patterns 33–4, 55
speed (tempo) 13–14, 61–2, 68, 96, 105
'Speed Music' 40
stories 5, 22, 75, 90, 94
strong beats 27–29
styles 22, 61, 89, 103, 105, 109
suite 93

timbre 5, 6, 8–10, 16, 46–7, 61, 90, 94
time 13, 28, 30, 33, 54–5, 73
time signatures 54–5
topic work 17, 22, 31, 113
transducer 46–7
transposing 60, 110
treble clef 54
tubular bells 115, 117
tuned percussion 17, 19, 24–6, 34–5, 38, 41, 66, 114
tunes 36, 42, 58, 60, 85, 89–90

violin 51, 60
visual art 86, 109
volume 15, 38, 64, 94, 113, 115

whole note 52
whole-tone scale 26, 123
wind chimes 118–19

xylophone 18, 32, 60, 67, 91, 115–17